THIS ROUGH MAGIC

BY HELEN MACHALIAS

CURRENCY PRESS
The performing arts publisher

CURRENT THEATRE SERIES

First published in 2023
by Currency Press
Gadigal Land, PO Box 2287 Strawberry Hills, NSW, 2012, Australia
enquiries@currency.com.au
www.currency.com.au

in association with The Street Theatre

Typeset by Brighton Gray for Currency Press.
Printed by Fineline Print + Copy Services, Revesby, NSW.
Cover Illustration and Design by Design♡Cult.
Inside Pages Photography by Novel Photographic.

Currency Press acknowledges the Traditional Owners of the Country on which we live and work. We pay our respects to all Aboriginal and Torres Strait Islander Elders, past and present.

A catalogue record for this book is available from the National Library of Australia

Contents

For Rey and Alex

This Rough Magic was first produced by The Street at The Street Theatre, Canberra, on the lands of the Ngunnawal and Ngambi peoples, on 11 November 2023, with the following cast:

PROSPERO	George Kanaan
ARIEL	Reza Momenzada
MIRANDA	Kaitlin Nihill
CALIBAN	Andre Le
DIVE-SHOP OWNER, THE OFFICIAL, PARNIA	Lainie Hart

POLITICIANS, the chorus of HUNGRY GHOSTS and REFUGEES are played by the ensemble.

Director, Beng Oh
Dramaturgs, Dr Rebecca Clode, Granaz Moussavi
Lighting Design, Gerry Corcoran
Production Design, Imogen Keen
Sound Design, Kyle Sheedy
Cultural Consultants, Sheida Jafari, Parastoo Seif
Stage Manager, Brittany Myers
Lighting Operaor, William Malam
Sound Operator, Kyle Sheedy
Set Construction, AVL Australia
Production Crew, Gerry Corcoran, Darren Hawkins, Connor McKay, William Malam

CHARACTERS

PROSPERO, middle-aged Iranian man, on island since shipwreck, assistant manager of island detention centre.

ARIEL, Iranian man in his 30s, on island since shipwreck.

MIRANDA, female Iranian in late teens, on island since shipwreck. She wears a Muslim headdress in Act 1, Scenes 1, 2 and 4.

CALIBAN, a Chinese-Malay man in his early 20s, born on island. Works as a guard on the Christmas Island detention centre following the shipwreck.

DIVE-SHOP OWNER, on island for past five years.

THE OFFICIAL (an immigration official), on island for past three months.

PARNIA, Iranian woman in her 30s, on island since shipwreck.

NOTES

The roles of DIVE-SHOP OWNER, PARNIA and THE OFFICIAL can be performed by the same actor. An interval may be held after Act 1.

THE POLITICIAN's dialogue is taken verbatim from Australian politicians. They can be presented by members of the ensemble cast or via audio recordings of the politicians.

When characters speak into the onstage microphone, they are communicating with Australia.

English translations for the Farsi, Chinese, Arabic and Malay spoken are provided in brackets. The play features text excerpts from Shakespeare's *The Tempest*, *Pericles* and *King Lear*, Hafiz's poetry, *Shahnameh*, *The Little Black Fish*, *The Conference of the Birds*, Rumi's poetry, *Hey You* by Nima Yushij and 'The Strangers' Case' from *Sir Thomas More*.

This play text went to press before the end of rehearsals and may differ from the play as performed.

ACT ONE: SEA-SORROW

SCENE ONE

A microphone in a stand is on stage. PROSPERO *enters, wearing a cloak and holding a staff and book.*

PROSPERO: It begins, as always, with a storm. Sit still, and hear of my sea-sorrow.

What follows is an account of PROSPERO, MIRANDA *and* ARIEL*'s arrival on the island told from multiple perspectives. The storm reaches a crescendo. Lines overlap throughout the scene in the chaos. Sirens sound continually.*

Ensemble cast enters, including CALIBAN, *running and holding a machete.*

CALIBAN: Life jackets!
DIVE-SHOP OWNER: How many?
CALIBAN: Reffo boat! / Sound the alarm.

PROSPERO *tries to command the waves using his staff.*

PROSPERO: Cease your ire, you angry stars of heaven.
CALIBAN: Where are the navy boats?
PROSPERO: Wind, rain, and thunder. / Earthly man is but a substance that must yield to you.
MIRANDA: Stand fast, good fate!
PROSPERO: 'Black night, our fear of the waves, and the horrible whirlpool.'
DIVE-SHOP OWNER: Nobody else get in the water! / You're making it worse.
CALIBAN: That swell must be four metres. / We need some help!
DIVE-SHOP OWNER: The ship's coming apart!
MIRANDA: Esteri!

Silence. The ship is lost.

DIVE-SHOP OWNER: Great tourist spot, this. Flying Fish Cove. You've picked the perfect spot to come diving. Crystal-clear waters.

Million-dollar views. Sharp rocks. Very sharp. Don't walk around here barefoot or in thongs. But we do.

What would you call the colour of the sea? It changes. Azure. Periwinkle. Cornflower. The fish have great names. Raccoon butterflyfish. Freckled hawkfish. Whitetail squirrelfish. Bluelined surgeonfish. The blackspotted pufferfish, so named because his face looks like a sea lion. Search me.

Hey, you got a good set of lungs on you? You'll have to hold your breath for a while. Hold your nerve. Big deep breath and hold.

The refugees take a collective breath.

Welcome to paradise.

CALIBAN *and* DIVE-SHOP OWNER *call down to the asylum seekers from the clifftop.*

CALIBAN: Get away from the cliffs! / Swim the other way!

DIVE-SHOP OWNER: Grab the life jacket! / Hang on to the life jacket! / What are they doing?

CALIBAN: Their screams woke the people who live on this road.

PROSPERO, *defeated, pulls himself to safety.*

PROSPERO: Alas, the seas have cast me on the rocks, washed me from shore to shore, and left me breath, nothing to think on but ensuing death.

CALIBAN: Only forty-two people rescued. And one man made it shore by himself.

DIVE-SHOP OWNER: Prospero. Not a local.

CALIBAN: He'd brought his daughter too. He didn't wait for her. All those parents sinking like anchors with their babies' arms around their necks.

DIVE-SHOP OWNER: But Prospero jumped from the boat as it hit the rock and pulled himself to safety.

PROSPERO: I would give a thousand furlongs of sea for an acre of barren ground. After today, I am determined to die a dry death.

DIVE-SHOP OWNER: [*into microphone*] Customs, the flying doctor service were all in there, getting in each other's way. Coppers were on the scene to round them all up. Tickets, please.

CALIBAN *intercepts a group of navy officials who are attempting to detain* MIRANDA.

THE OFFICIAL: Move to the side now.

CALIBAN: Get off her, babi setan (devil pig). She can hardly breathe. Leave her be, she's not going anywhere.

The officials stand guard close to MIRANDA *and* CALIBAN.

MIRANDA: Nemitounam babamo bebeenam. (I cannot see my dad.)

CALIBAN: You nearly drowned. / Sit down while the paramedics get here.

MIRANDA: Donbal e babam migardam. (I'm looking for my dad.)

CALIBAN: I can't understand you. / Here, take this blanket.

MIRANDA: [*to audience*] A brave vessel, dashed to pieces. Their cries knock against my heart. We imagined a hopeful beginning. Not this.

DIVE-SHOP OWNER: [*to audience*] Cameras everywhere. Why would anyone want to see this on telly while you're eating your dinner?

The arrivals blink from the flashes of media cameras. As the unused life jackets are collected, THE POLITICIAN *(Chris Bowen) speaks:*

THE POLITICIAN: I must say I think the hardest part actually came the next day when I got the information that babies had died, a two-month old and an eight-month old, and I had to tell the Prime Minister that, and that was obviously hard for her and a hard conversation for anybody to have to be outlining just the full devastation that we were dealing with ... There happened to be TV cameras there to capture this tragedy and show the Australian people about it. It may have happened since Christmas Island and we don't know about it. And that's what's really confronting about this and really ... really does worry me. And that's what drives me, and I think drives the Government to keep us focused on trying to discourage boat journeys to Australia.

SCENE TWO

A few hours later. PROSPERO *and* MIRANDA *are waiting to be interviewed.*

PROSPERO: Be collected. Tell your piteous heart there's no harm done. Do you remember a time before we came into this cell?

MIRANDA: I ...

PROSPERO: It's important you pretend that you do. Today, they will expect you to tell them what it was like before.

MIRANDA: Our prayer centre was attacked. They imprisoned our leaders. Sufis were banned from government jobs, so my father couldn't work—

PROSPERO: Too much detail. Don't make it political. Focus on your education, how it impacted you as a child.

MIRANDA: I couldn't go to school anymore.

PROSPERO: Make it dramatic.

MIRANDA: I'm tired.

PROSPERO: You need to practise. Where are you from?

MIRANDA: Iran.

PROSPERO: Where did you board the ship?

MIRANDA: I don't know. We had been travelling a long time already.

PROSPERO: What were you told about the journey?

MIRANDA: Nothing.

PROSPERO: Why did you leave Iran?

MIRANDA: Because we weren't safe. Sufi families were being p—

PROSPERO: Persecuted. Our family was being persecuted. Why did you come to Australia?

MIRANDA: Because Australia welcomes refugees.

PROSPERO: Big eyes when you say that, appeal to them.

MIRANDA: Because Australia welcomes refugees.

PROSPERO: [*to audience*] It helps to have a child. If they say the right thing.

MIRANDA: How did we reach this shore?

PROSPERO: God's willing. Our escape is much beyond our loss.

MIRANDA: Did you know I'd need to swim? Is that why you taught me in Kish?

PROSPERO: Never mention the journey. Don't remind them how we came here.

MIRANDA: How could anyone who saw the boat be angry with us? That boat frightened me.

PROSPERO: No-one could have predicted it.

MIRANDA: We should have waited for another boat.

PROSPERO: [*to audience*] They hurried us aboard a barge, and carried us miles out to sea, where they had prepared a rotten carcass of a boat, with no sails or masts or ropes—even the rats had the sense to abandon it. They tossed us in the water to cry to the sea that roared back at us, to sigh into the winds that shrieked back at us in pity. [*To* MIRANDA] There was no other boat. For the miracle of our preservation, few can speak like us. Then wisely, my Miranda, weigh our sorrow with our comfort.

SCENE THREE

February 2011. Two months after the shipwreck. ARIEL *waits to be interviewed, holding a white funeral shroud. An interview between* THE POLITICIAN *(Scott Morrison) and* JOURNALIST *(Barbara Miller).*

THE POLITICIAN: This is a government whose failed border protection policies has increased the cost of asylum seeker management by more than sevenfold in just the last three years. They need to understand the value of taxpayers' dollars in this area.

JOURNALIST: Scott Morrison says it's not reasonable for the Government to cover the costs of holding the funerals in Sydney.

THE POLITICIAN: The Government had the option of having these services on Christmas Island. If relatives of those who were involved wanted to go to Christmas Island, like any other Australian who wanted to attend a funeral service in another part of the country, they would have made their own arrangements to be there.

JOURNALIST: Do you think you run the risk of being seen as heartless on the day of these funerals to be saying … to be bickering over this money?

THE POLITICIAN: Well you're asking the questions and I'm answering them. And when it comes to the question of do I think this is a reasonable cost, then my honest answer is, no I don't think it is reasonable.

> ARIEL *is startled to see an immigration official (*THE OFFICIAL*) appear via video.*

THE OFFICIAL: Starting recording for interview on Monday fourteenth February 2011 with detainee SIEV two-two-one-twenty in relation to deceased detainee SIEV two-two-one-twenty-two. So, you've requested special consideration in relation to the funeral of your daughter Esteri?

ARIEL: Yes. She cannot be given a funeral in Sydney. That is not her mother's … that is not our wish.

THE OFFICIAL: The funeral is currently scheduled for the twentieth of February, is that correct?

ARIEL: Yes.

THE OFFICIAL: How old was Esteri when she died?

ARIEL: Eight months old.

THE OFFICIAL: Eight months old. And has she been kept on the island?

ARIEL: Yes. In a fridge.

THE OFFICIAL: Not a fridge, it's a secure chilled storage hold at the morgue. But yes. You haven't seen her? Since—

ARIEL: No, we're not permitted. Two months she's been there. At home, we bury the dead as soon as possible, to respect the body.

THE OFFICIAL: And on what grounds are you challenging the location of the funeral?

ARIEL: Compassionate grounds.

THE OFFICIAL: The options are religious, medical, human rights or legal. So which one would you like?

ARIEL: Religious.

THE OFFICIAL: Okay, religious appeal.

ARIEL: Because she can't be buried like that.

THE OFFICIAL: The notes say she's getting a Muslim burial.

ARIEL: It's a Muslim ceremony, in some respects, but not all the traditions are being observed. So I want her buried in Iran.

THE OFFICIAL: Iran?

ARIEL: Yes.

THE OFFICIAL: That you've just left, saying you feared for your lives?

ARIEL: Yes.

THE OFFICIAL: You'd return to Iran for her funeral?

ARIEL: No. It still isn't safe for us. But I have family there. They'd bury her properly.

THE OFFICIAL: What would that involve?

ARIEL: Esteri's body needs to be washed at a mosque and buried in a cloth without a casket. I have asked for this many times, and been told no. Holding her body, saying goodbye to her, that is very important to us.

A buzz of distorted audio and THE OFFICIAL *is gone.* ARIEL *holds the white shroud.*

SCENE FOUR

March 2011. Three months after the shipwreck. Elegiac Persian music plays as the ensemble gathers. ARIEL *enters and tenderly arranges a white cloth on the floor.*

ARIEL: [*repeating*] Chera Rafti? (Why did you go?) Esteri. Khodaya! (Oh God!)

PROSPERO *enters, holding a staff and begins recounting a story from Shahnameh.*

PROSPERO: The prophet's grandson Imam Hussain could not see a way out of his troubles. He was surrounded, outnumbered by heartless men, while his family and companions were slain like sacrificial lambs. For days all he could hear was the crying and wailing of the children and women, and he knew he must do something to change their situation. He addressed the group.

ARIEL: [*to group*] Where is the protector who can defend the sanctity of Hussain? Where are the believers, even as we suffer with what befalls us? Where is a deliverer who aspires to be rewarded for alleviating our distress?

[*To Esteri*] It is not a simple decision to leave your home. But we did not recognise our home anymore. We waited until you were born, and then we began to make arrangements. A lot of planning, a lot of failures. And then, an opportunity.

Throughout the scene a chorus of women's voices responds to PROSPERO *and* ARIEL, *led by* PARNIA *and* MIRANDA, *the keening and wailing continually undulating under* PROSPERO *and* ARIEL*'s dialogue.*

PROSPERO: Hussain told his family to stop crying because he knew what to do. He asked for his infant child so he could kiss the baby before he embarked on his mission. He told the child 'Away with those enemies! For I, the chosen Imam, will be their enemy on the day of judgment'.

PARNIA/MIRANDA: Bemeeram baraat. (I wish I were killed instead of you.)

ARIEL: So many times during the journey we were in danger. I would hold you, and if it wasn't safe to have you at my chest, I would lift you up, up, up in my arms, away from it all. When we saw the navy boats, the smugglers said 'Quick, quick, put the children in the air, show them there are children on board'.

PARNIA/MIRANDA: Chera rafti? (Why did you go?)

ARIEL *lifts the white cloth above his head.*

PROSPERO: Hussain lifted the baby high above his head and asked for the enemy to have mercy and provide water for the parched child to drink. Harmalah bin Kahil al-Azdi instead shot the infant through the neck with an arrow.

ARIEL: I kept you high out of the water for as long as I could.

PARNIA/MIRANDA: Esteri. Khodaya! (Oh God!)

PROSPERO: The baby hovered between life and death, its breath coming in unsteady gasps. Hussain held the child's hand, and this touch was like a magic wand.

ARIEL: Then you were gone.

THE POLITICIAN *(John Howard) speaks.*

THE POLITICIAN: I do not want people in Australia who would throw their own children into the sea. I don't. There's something incompatible to me about people who claim to be refugees and someone who would throw their own child into the sea, it offends the natural instincts of protection, and delivering security and safety to your children.

PARNIA/MIRANDA: Khodaya, che konaam? (Oh God, what do I do now?)

PROSPERO: A smile appeared on the baby's face, to tell 'Worry not Father, all is well'. With his steady hand, Hussain dug a sandy grave. An emotion's tempest, though did blow, not solitary tear, his grief did show. This precious gift to Islam he gave of an infant martyr, whose blood was not spilled in vain.

PARNIA/MIRANDA: Koja rafti? (Where did you go?)

ARIEL, PROSPERO *and others beat their chests in mourning. The percussive effect of the beating blends with the sound of the ocean.* PROSPERO *holds a seashell to his ear, then hands it to* ARIEL.

PROSPERO: Your daughter. She tells you, 'Worry not, Father, all is well'.

PROSPERO *and* ARIEL *move away from the scene of the funeral,* ARIEL *still holding the seashell,* PROSPERO *holding his book of Hafiz poetry.*

All are fruits of one tree and leaves of one branch.

ARIEL *places his hand in* PROSPERO*'s to commence the bay'ah ceremony (oath of allegiance), which initiates* ARIEL *into the Sufi order and commits* ARIEL *to* PROSPERO, *his spiritual master.*

ARIEL: 'We need a judge of rare ability
To lead us over danger's spacious sea;
Whatever he commands along the Way,
We must, without recalcitrance, obey.'

PROSPERO: 'To the limit that you can carry.
One who suffers and is guided gives
His merit to the world; he truly lives.
Take refuge in the orders of your guide,
And like a slave subdue your restive pride.'

ARIEL *crosses his arms so his hands rest on his shoulders and kisses a hand of* PROSPERO*'s folded arms.* ARIEL *follows* PROSPERO*'s lead and prostrates himself in prayer. They pray silently for a moment, then* ARIEL *returns to the embrace of the assembled mourners.*

SCENE FIVE

April 2011. Four months after the shipwreck. CALIBAN *and* MIRANDA *are at the clifftops at Esteri's grave.* CALIBAN *is in a guard's uniform, a baton hanging from his belt.* MIRANDA *is sharing a story with* CALIBAN *and Esteri.*

MIRANDA: Once upon a time, a little black fish lived as an only child with her mother in a tiny pond.

The little black fish wanted more than anything to see the moonlight, just once. Early one morning, the little black fish woke her mother before sunrise and said 'Mother, I want to talk to you'.

The mother said 'Child, it's too early to talk. Go swimming until I wake up'.

'I can't swim anymore', the little black fish said. 'I must leave here.'

'Where are you going this hour of the morning?' asked the mother.

The little black fish explained 'I want to go and find where the stream ends. I want to know what happens in other places'.

The mother said 'Darling heart, I used to wonder the same thing when I was a child. But, a stream has no beginning and no end. The stream just flows and doesn't go anywhere'.

But the little black fish would not be persuaded. 'I'm tired of swimming. I want to know what's happening elsewhere. I want to know if life is simply for circling around in a small place until you are old, or if there is another way to be in this world?'

The mother let the little black fish finish. 'My sweet child, are you crazy? What is this other world? The world is right here. Life is just as we have it.'

Beat.

Ariel and Parnia have not visited Esteri's grave yet.

CALIBAN: Let me know when they want to come. I can bring them up here for their hour. Then take them back.

MIRANDA: I'll tell them.

Beat.

The stars are above, wherever we are. This is a most majestic vision.

CALIBAN: I can show you every part of this island. All the secret paths. The best caves to swim in. Where the whale sharks live. The wild food that's good to eat, and the food that's poisonous. The best places to hide and watch. Here, I've got something to show you.

CALIBAN *produces a glass jar with glowing fireflies in it.*

MIRANDA: They're beautiful. Are they happy in there?

CALIBAN: I'll need to release them soon. Back in the day my ah-kong (grandfather) would light the mines with these. But he couldn't figure out how to keep the fireflies alive for longer than a couple of days. So he uses phosphorescent dried fish skin now. Looks wicked.

MIRANDA: How long have these ones been in the jar?

CALIBAN: Ten days. A record. Ah-Kong's friend Akio told him not to bring them into the mines because they're the souls of the dead. Brings bad luck.

MIRANDA: Are they the souls of the dead?

CALIBAN: They're the spirits of samurai. Warriors killed in battle. There are so many things that glow around here. Flashlight fish. Vampire squid. Lantern sharks.

MIRANDA: Would there have been lantern sharks in the water when we came?

CALIBAN: No, they're wimps. Hate choppy water. They wouldn't have gone near the bodies. The people. Don't worry about that.

Beat.

The jungle floors here glow at night, too. Some nights, the seawater sparks. Like when you rub sticks together. You can see it from up here on the clifftop. I'll show you sometime.

Beat.

Mum's been asking me about you.

MIRANDA: What's she been asking?

CALIBAN: She noticed you weren't wearing your hijab anymore. Did you have to fight your dad for that?

MIRANDA: No, he encouraged me. [*Imitates Prospero*] We must look as Australian as possible.

CALIBAN: I reckon you two would get along. You and Mum.

MIRANDA: Why?

CALIBAN: You're both pretty badass.

MIRANDA: What?

CALIBAN: You're both like torch lights.

MIRANDA: I think I know what you mean.

CALIBAN: I can't get over how good my pay is. Mum is so proud I'm working for the government. I told her it's only a contract gig, but she reckons if I work hard, I'll be set for life. I'm gonna get a new dishwasher for Mum. She's been telling me she likes washing dishes by hand, but she does enough of that at work. So, I'll sort that next month.

Beat.

This is a good spot to let the fireflies go. You do it.

MIRANDA *opens the jar and releases the fireflies, who glimmer in the night sky. Sirens blare.*

CALIBAN: Curfew. Time to take you home.

MIRANDA: My one hour of freedom over. Same place next week?

CALIBAN *nods.* MIRANDA *exits.*

CALIBAN: [*to himself*] The instant that I saw you my heart flew to your service. There it resides to make me slave for it.

SCENE SIX

May 2011. Six months after the shipwreck. While PARNIA *and* PROSPERO *talk,* MIRANDA *prepares espand seeds for heating.*

PARNIA: The humidity, it is not good for my lungs.

PROSPERO: The phosphate. The toxic dust makes the roads slippery. Imagine what it is doing to our bodies.

PARNIA: May Satan be blind, may Satan be deaf. I pray we will leave here soon.

PROSPERO: Hush. There are few trusted friends here, and the whole island has a dark magic. Don't speak your dreams aloud.

PARNIA: You believe the tales? Surely the guards are just trying to scare us.

PROSPERO: The espand, Miranda.

MIRANDA *brings over the smoking pan of espand seeds.* PROSPERO *fans the smoke over* PARNIA.

Your lungs are now cleansed. The phosphate has gone from them. Your cough will trouble you no more.

PROSPERO *blows his breath into* PARNIA*'s face for good luck.*

Blessings to you, Ariel and Aayaan.

PARNIA: I dreamt I was in a cave on this island. Stalactites hung from the ceiling and the shrieking of bats blended with the screams of dead islanders.

The sounds of the island infiltrate the space. PARNIA, MIRANDA *and* PROSPERO *shudder.*

You understand dreams. What did you see in your dream of enlightenment?

PROSPERO: It is as if you asked me 'Molecules are made of atoms—can you show me the atoms?' It would not be possible. So it is with Sufism. But Ariel is an excellent follower. I was not so loyal to my own murshid.

PARNIA: It would be better if Ariel spent more time with you rather than that revolutionary Ehsan.

PROSPERO: And Ehsan's wife, Roya—

PARNIA: Yes. I know.

PROSPERO: It is a mistake to associate with people just because they're Iranian. I pray you mark me, Miranda.

MIRANDA *indicates assent.*

But we do all share the wisdom of Hafiz. Let's hear what he has for you.

PARNIA *breathes on the book and opens it to a random page.*

PARNIA: O Hâfiz of Shîrâz, impart foreknowledge to my anxious heart.

PROSPERO: [*reading from the book*] 'For a long time my Beloved no message sent
Didn't write a greeting, and no word sent
I sent a hundred letters, yet that mounted King
Dispatched no messages, no greeting sent.' This is about—

MIRANDA: Ariel. He—

PROSPERO: Let me see your coffee cup.

PROSPERO *examines* PARNIA*'s cup.*

You've had a terrible journey, but I see no such darkness in your future. A trial, a test while you're here, and then prosperity and peace.

PARNIA: I cannot imagine a future from this place. Forever waiting for the next terrible thing—

PROSPERO: The paths of God are intricate and strange. Miranda has the gift too, let her check for you in the water.

MIRANDA *and* PARNIA *apply kohl eyeliner to each other's eyes to help them see into the future, and* MIRANDA *peers into the bowl of water while* PARNIA *places a sheet over her.* PROSPERO *addresses the audience, unheard by* MIRANDA *and* PARNIA.

I brought three books with me to this island.
My real life preservers, to vouchsafe our passage to Australia.
The first, the *Book of Kings*. This book saved our language, defines our people. As we are all stateless, you may ask, what does nationalism matter? But it matters. And I have always been able to make people love me through my stories.

This book also has my shajara (family tree). It links me to my clan, tracing back all the way to Chalabi, through descendants linked through their powers of mysticism.

The second book I brought is the poems of Hafiz. The wisdom embodied in these pages lights the way forward for us when we desperately need comfort.

'I'm not a traveller, but it never fails
To give me pleasure when I tell their tales;
It's just a taste of sweetness, I'm aware,
But better that than having poison here.'

But my third book is the most important one. I started writing it in Indonesia, helping asylum seekers to obtain new papers. I speak better English than anyone, so I put people's cases, make requests on their behalf.

They would tell me all the details of their lives before, and I take the notes down, choosing which parts of their story to include and what is better removed. Two versions of the truth. Version one is what they've told me, and version two is what I translate for Immigration.

'My book's all madness, Reason won't appear
Within its pages, she's a stranger here …
And when they say: Lost wanderer, it's you
You must ask pardon from for what you do,'
I don't know where to turn, since who could give
Forgiveness to the hundred lives I live?
If I were on His Way now, would I be
Drowned as I am in all this poetry?'

MIRANDA *re-enters after farewelling* PARNIA.

MIRANDA: Always the same dreams, of the caves. The caves call people to them.

PROSPERO: Don't you ever go into those caves. Tourists disappear in them.

Here, take these notes to Ariel. Tell him to remove the first two paragraphs, and then code paragraphs three, four, seven and eight for me to put into the book.

MIRANDA: You're giving me dangerous work. What will happen if a guard stops me?

PROSPERO: Not so dangerous. They shouldn't suspect a child.

MIRANDA: Not a child.

PROSPERO: And if they ask, you're going to see our friends Ariel and Parnia and looking after Aayaan. Who could be suspicious of those eyes?

MIRANDA: What is in these papers is very precious to the government. I'll do it today, but you should ask the Syrians next time.

PROSPERO: I can't trust those gangsters with this. You're helping people with their cases, Miranda. They searched my books beforehand when we arrived, what happened?

MIRANDA: Nothing.

PROSPERO: Nothing, exactly. Ariel and I hide the meaning of the words. Keeps us safe, keeps the others safe. Bring the book directly back to me once Ariel has finished. Go carefully, dokhmal.

MIRANDA *exits.*

SCENE SEVEN

August 2011. The sun is setting. The island's annual hungry ghosts festival is on. The gates of hell are opened and ghosts are free to roam the earth, where they seek food and entertainment. The DIVE-SHOP OWNER *is inside a cave secretly watching* PROSPERO, *who is holding his book and anticipating someone's arrival.* DIVE-SHOP OWNER *addresses the audience, unheard by* PROSPERO.

DIVE-SHOP OWNER: It's an interesting spot to have chosen for a 'regional processing centre'. Australia, but without Australia's rules.

Don't let the hunger strikes fool you, they've made themselves very comfortable in eight months. I wouldn't turn my nose up at a buffet lunch and dinner every day.

A lot of people helped when the boat crashed. Which was the right thing to do. But I think some people thought that should have been the end of it. The government should be turning people back, not letting more in. Maybe those fat cats in Canberra need to pay the big four a few more dirty millions to explain what 'border control' means.

A lot of them are nice enough, but it's the up and down we hate. This place looks like a high security prison these days. Yes, there's more jobs going, but we'd just like the tourists back.

DIVE-SHOP OWNER *moves towards* PROSPERO.

What the Flying Fish Cove are you doing here?

PROSPERO: I've heard strange tales about the caves. I came to see them myself.

DIVE-SHOP OWNER: What sort of strange tales?

PROSPERO: 'A most strange history, and a tale of marvels.'

DIVE-SHOP OWNER: That's not an answer.

PROSPERO: It's a quote.

DIVE-SHOP OWNER: People like you make it their business to talk in riddles. Think it makes them sound clever.

PROSPERO: I'm familiar with the business you're in—

DIVE-SHOP OWNER: I run a dive shop, mate.

PROSPERO: Fortune smiles on you. You have a thriving business, while the other islanders struggle.

DIVE-SHOP OWNER: Don't play cute. I know those Syrians tell you everything.

PROSPERO: Do you expect them to be loyal to you?

Beat.

The Syrians aren't familiar with your schedule. I didn't realise we'd be crossing over. It will be awkward to have me here for the exchange you're about to make, surely.

DIVE-SHOP OWNER: Sorry, did I not send you a calendar invite with the booking? You've been here two seconds, and you think this cave's yours now? All of you freeloaders, sucking the life out of this island.

PROSPERO: What was here before, that you're so proud of? A settlement of tax avoiders, criminals, drug dealers. With your Australian flags flying out the front of your tasteless houses, and everywhere a vagueness of morality. And you look down on us.

Beat.

I arrived here first. You go.

PROSPERO *makes a summoning gesture and the overlapping voices of* HUNGRY GHOSTS *enter the cave.*

HUNGRY GHOST ONE: Forgotten ancestors / rising from diyu (hell), come to feast.

HUNGRY GHOST TWO: A maze of chambers / to punish souls for sins.

HUNGRY GHOST THREE: Burn the joss paper / and make rice from the burning coal.

HUNGRY GHOST ONE: Xiāng guǒ tán zài nǎlǐ? (Where is the altar of incense and fruit?)

HUNGRY GHOST FOUR: Two stars max / Don't expect a cheap feed / Dark tourism / Lucky the booze and smokes are tax free.

HUNGRY GHOST TWO: No Australian style wining and dining / Mosquitos eating you alive / Island time.

DIVE-SHOP OWNER: The new master you're waiting for. I'll say their name.

PROSPERO *hushes* DIVE-SHOP OWNER.

PROSPERO: You cannot. This cave repeats what it hears.

The HUNGRY GHOSTS *hiss angrily.*

DIVE-SHOP OWNER: Hey, easy now. I just wanted to talk to you. So you think you know how to stop the riots and hunger strikes?

PROSPERO: I want to help. Make it a better place to live for everyone.

DIVE-SHOP OWNER: Noble sentiments, Mr P. All islands are trading places. What will you trade? Your girl?

The HUNGRY GHOSTS *move towards* PROSPERO, *who hurriedly lights incense to disperse them.* PROSPERO *acts out an exchange between* DIVE-SHOP OWNER *and* THE OFFICIAL.

PROSPERO: [*as* THE OFFICIAL] You need to watch what you're giving them. Nothing that makes them aggro.

[*As* DIVE-SHOP OWNER] I'm not gonna bring crank into the camp, I promised you that.

[*As* THE OFFICIAL]: The guards don't know their arse from their elbow. Hopefully this other option works. The guy knows everything.

[*As* DIVE-SHOP OWNER] He looks straighty one-eighty to me. I don't need someone taking the moral high ground on island life.

DIVE-SHOP OWNER: Not your first time in the cave, huh?

Beat.

I used to be great mates with the old administrator. This new one won't last long. They think it's a cushy job. They enjoy the warm weather, then back to the mainland for truffle parmesan fries or some shit.

PROSPERO: This has been the strangest interview I've had on this island.

Beat.

I won't interfere with your trade.

DIVE-SHOP OWNER: I don't go much on people's promises.

Beat.

What's the deal with the book?

PROSPERO: Just stories from home.

DIVE-SHOP OWNER: You're hanging on very tight. Give it here, then.

DIVE-SHOP OWNER *lunges to wrench the book from* PROSPERO*'s hand. As they tussle, the book opens, loose sheets of paper fall on the floor, and the overlapping, blended voices of different refugees speaking in various languages are heard simultaneously, alongside* PROSPERO*'s description of the book.*

VOICE A: My home was demolished / In the beginning / Unforgiving / I heard screaming.

VOICE B: Man dar khafa kar mikardam (I worked secretly) / zendegim dar khatar bood (life in imminent danger) / zanam ghargh shod (my wife drowned).

VOICE C: Suaka (asylum) / keluarga yang sakit (sick family) / penentang (dissidents) / manusia tetapi tidak kelihatan (human but invisible).

VOICE D: 'If you're a person who can seek, do so, /
Give up your soul, find what you long to know /
And if you sniff my ocean, in this flood /
Of poetry you'll certainly smell blood / '

PROSPERO: 'But I weep tears of blood for verse, and bleed them /
To shed blood in the hearts of those who read /
them,
And people's falsehood poisons need but look /
For poison's antidote within my book.'

PROSPERO *slams the book shut and gathers up the loose sheets of paper.*

DIVE-SHOP OWNER: Snitching on your friends, are you?

PROSPERO: We're genuine refugees. We should have been granted asylum already.

DIVE-SHOP OWNER: That's what everyone says. You can't all be right.

PROSPERO: No. Not everyone.

DIVE-SHOP OWNER: None of my business, mate. Some free advice. Now that we're friends. Ask 'em for twelve months in exchange. Too quick and it looks dodgy. Too long and … well, you're living here. You need an actual gig. So you have a reason for the detainees to keep telling you things. Get them to throw in school for your girl.

Beat.

I would like one thing from you. One letter. From that special book of yours.

PROSPERO: They're coded. They're not of any value to you.

DIVE-SHOP OWNER: But they're of value to you. Would be a nice way of showing that we're partners in this enterprise.

PROSPERO: Someone else is expecting them.

DIVE-SHOP OWNER: Christ, this is amateur hour. Don't give them your whole supply at once, yeah? You portion it out. And you give me one. For your security. In case they take them all.

PROSPERO *considers.*

Or I can just take the whole thing now.

PROSPERO *flicks through the book, selects a letter and reluctantly tears a sheet of paper from the book and gives it to* DIVE-SHOP OWNER.

Who does this letter belong to?

PROSPERO: Ehsan. He writes lots of letters for Ariel.

DIVE-SHOP OWNER *motions to put his hand out to* PROSPERO, *who goes to shake it, before* DIVE-SHOP OWNER *takes his hand away.*

DIVE-SHOP OWNER: Gotcha.

DIVE-SHOP OWNER *exits.*

SCENE EIGHT

March 2012. Fifteen months after the shipwreck. Prospero's quarters. MIRANDA *is preparing food. The smells of browning butter, saffron, cooking rice and smoked fish fill the air.* ARIEL *pauses at the entrance, inhaling deeply before entering.*

ARIEL: Sabzi polo ba mahi? (Herb rice with fish?)

PROSPERO: Miranda's favourite.

MIRANDA: Let's share it together.

ARIEL: You're celebrating Nowruz?

MIRANDA: Of course.

PROSPERO: I felt like eating the dish and procured some saffron. Please, join us.

MIRANDA: Have you had food from home since you arrived?

ARIEL: No.

MIRANDA: Sit down, please. It's nearly ready.

PROSPERO: Certainly a time to celebrate. Everything is running smoothly. My spells are not breaking. We are safe.

PROSPERO *registers Ariel's mood.*

What is it? Something at camp? Is it Parnia?

ARIEL: No, no. Not Parnia. I wanted to ask you something.

MIRANDA: Will the others want to celebrate Nowruz? I could organise flowers? [*Playfully*] Fire jumping might not be allowed.

PROSPERO: What foolishness, Miranda. These people don't want flowers.

ARIEL: They don't want fire, either.

PROSPERO: I am glad to hear it.

ARIEL: You are fortunate to have been granted a measure of freedom.

PROSPERO: I help out a bit more around camp, so I get some little rewards, like this accommodation. But our case still hasn't been decided.

MIRANDA: We're not staying here, are we?

ARIEL: I'm sure many people would love this accommodation.

PROSPERO: You should have seen my home before. What are you demanding of me?

ARIEL: Not demanding. Requesting my liberty.

PROSPERO: Your time's not done yet.

ARIEL: They're reconsidering my application.

PROSPERO: Because I intervened on your behalf. Things were not looking good for you.

ARIEL: If I had an appointment that was longer than fifteen minutes, I could persuade them. Can't you do more?

PROSPERO: Just a little while longer, and you will be as free as mountain winds.

ARIEL: Being here is harmful for my family. I need a definite date, to give to Parnia.

PROSPERO: I pray for your wife's return to health, but now is not the time to be pushy with them. She should not have participated in the hunger strike. I told you that.

ARIEL: I have shown great loyalty to you, never lied to you, served you secretly, without complaint. And you promised me that you would make arrangements for me to go to Australia. Yet I'm still here.

PROSPERO: Your time is not out yet. I've already helped with your passage from Indonesia.

ARIEL: Areh vali nemeetounam ta abad sabr konam— (Yes, but I cannot wait forever—)

PROSPERO: You know I don't speak Farsi in front of my daughter. Her English is excellent, and I will not undo her progress.

ARIEL: Nothing makes me prouder than to hear my son speak Farsi. Surely the loyalty I have shown to you, our shared history—

PROSPERO: History, history, everyone is obsessed with their history.
'Come, why should you be dealing harshly with me—
Something is due for our old companionship's sake.'

ARIEL: Ehsan has asked me to speak to you. They don't believe his story. He cannot budge till your release.

PROSPERO: A violent man.

ARIEL: He retaliated. They beat him.

PROSPERO: The guards claimed it was self-defence.

PROSPERO *gestures to* ARIEL.

It is hard enough to secure the freedom of the ones who behave.

ARIEL: Please, you have been where he has been. You know—

PROSPERO: I did not hit guards. Because I knew that discipline would grant me a new life. Can you see that if you or I intervene we will be stained by association?

ARIEL: Help Ehsan, it's the right thing to do. The officials know that he lied about the work he used to do.

PROSPERO: Foolish to tell unnecessary lies. I told him that.

ARIEL: He was trying to make a stronger case for his skills. But now they know he was an agricultural worker. Have you kept the book safe?

PROSPERO: Of course I have. But that's all I can do for him.

ARIEL: It is a desperate situation, be human.

PROSPERO: If my daughter gives you some of her cookies, will you stop asking?

ARIEL: I don't want sweets. I'm going to arrange the release of the sabzeh sprouts on the beach for a group of us tomorrow. Remember to make your wish, Miranda.

MIRANDA: That's easy, I—

PROSPERO: Don't speak it out aloud.

ARIEL: Let people have their dreams, Prospero.

ARIEL *exits.*

MIRANDA: If Ehsan needs our help—

PROSPERO: Remember, I've done nothing but for care of you.

SCENE NINE

The next day. The sounds of humid lushness under the forest canopy. CALIBAN, *holding a machete, is watching* MIRANDA *tie sabzeh sprouts by a stream.*

MIRANDA: I know you're there, Caliban.

CALIBAN: You've got eyes in the back of your head, now?

MIRANDA: The birds behave differently when you're around.

CALIBAN: Really?

MIRANDA: You're also terrible at keeping quiet.

CALIBAN: What are you doing?

MIRANDA: New Year's wish. I need to finish tying this up and put it in the water.

CALIBAN: You haven't done those knots properly, let me give you a hand.
MIRANDA: This is just for me.
CALIBAN: Go on, it'll take me two seconds.
MIRANDA: Leave it, I said. You'll get phosphate dust on it.
CALIBAN: [*dusting off his hands*] I was helping Ah-Kong (Grandfather). I'll glow in the dark later. Sorry.

MIRANDA *places the tied sabzeh sprouts in the stream. An awkward pause.*

MIRANDA: You'd better take me back. We'll both be in trouble if I'm late.
CALIBAN: You're always worried.

MIRANDA *moves away.*

Wait, I want to show you the caves again.
MIRANDA: I don't want to go there again.

Beat.

You should get out of here, get a proper job.
CALIBAN: I like my job.

MIRANDA *is unconvinced.*

Money's good. Meet interesting people.

Beat.

Have you got trees like this at home? Tahitian chestnut tree.
MIRANDA: We don't have Tahitian chestnut trees in Iran, no.
CALIBAN: Don't disturb the roots. They'll wrap around you and hold you down. And then you'll really be stuck here.

A long pause.

You don't need to stress, you're still a virgin.
MIRANDA: I trusted you.
CALIBAN: You can still trust me.

Another long pause.

Have you told anyone? Don't tell your dad. I'd lose my job.
MIRANDA: I'm not going to tell anyone.
CALIBAN: I stopped when you yelled at me. And I like you. That's why I take you to nice places, like the waterfall.

MIRANDA: We'll go to the mainland soon, do you understand?
CALIBAN: Everything's here.
MIRANDA: I can have more than this in Australia.
CALIBAN: You have big dreams.
MIRANDA: We didn't come this far for life in a camp.

Beat.

But this week, Australia's felt very far away.

Pause.

The time, it's too late. It's the time between afternoon and night—
CALIBAN: Dusk. Most romantic time of day. I have a surprise for you.

CALIBAN *reaches into his backpack.*

MIRANDA: Wahoo fish! It tastes like—
CALIBAN: The fish back home. For the last day of Nowruz.
MIRANDA: It's so big. How did you catch it?
CALIBAN: I told him it was safe to jump into my net, and the silly bugger trusted me. Come on, I'll take you and him home.

SCENE TEN

May 2012. Seventeen months after the shipwreck. ARIEL *addresses the audience.*

ARIEL: The air breathes upon us here as if it had lungs. Rotten ones. There is everything here advantageous to life. Save means to live.

Crabs cover every inch of this decaying island. Forever walking sideways. They scurry over you as you sleep and nip your toes in the shower. They're always together and if you try and grab one, the others rise up against you and overpower you until you let their friend drop. They know I'm an intruder, so they do as they please.

Whatever is happening on the island, words are still magic.

Prospero tells me, lance the wound, let them pour their unhappiness into your paper, rather than spread it through camp. So I collect the stories. Prospero knows about that.

But then I send the letters I like off to the mainland. I'm working with people who help refugees by sharing our stories. Little bombs to detonate on Australian soil. Prospero doesn't know about that.

My letters have caused quite a storm in Australia. The letters written by Ehsan are the ones everyone wants to hear.

Sound of phone dialling as ARIEL *speaks into microphone back to Australia, reading from Ehsan's letter.*

It has been eighteen months since we arrived, and no-one is in a proper mental condition. People keep trying to kill themselves. Cutting wrists with razors. The girl who ate washing powder, it caused her big problems in her lungs. My neighbour stopped eating and sewed her lips together.

ARIEL *stops reading, pained.*

Ehsan writes about Parnia. She … well, as Ehsan says. Her lips are still very tender.

ARIEL *returns to the letter.*

Parents don't have any solution to improve the situation and every day we have to answer our children asking 'Why are we in prison and have not been set free?'

A voiceover from THE POLITICIAN *(Tony Abbott) is heard.*

THE POLITICIAN: Don't forget, Jesus drove the traitors from the temple as well … Jesus didn't say yes to everyone. I mean, Jesus knew that there was a place for everything and it is not necessarily everyone's place to come to Australia.

ARIEL *alternates between recounting the story to a group of attentive fellow refugees and sharing this story with journalists.*

ARIEL: [*to journalists*] This island is deliberately uninhabitable and inaccessible. Your country has begun a new age of slavery. A barbarian age with a cruel dictator government.

Officers look at us angrily, they give us the feeling we are criminals and murderers. Your immigration behave like we are ignorant and stupid animals, like sheep.

ARIEL *carefully folds Ehsan's letter and puts it into* PROSPERO*'s book as he shares his memories of the shipwreck.*

[*To journalists*] Everyone wants to know about the shipwreck. 'The worst civilian maritime disaster in Australia in more than a century.' A ship no stronger than a nutshell and leaking like a sieve.

Prospero was chanting, calling to the waves to stop. But the black smoke kept billowing and the engine failed twice. I had some seafaring experience from growing up fishing in Chah Bahar, so I took charge.

[*To assembled group*] When the ship broke up, everyone but the smugglers and the mothers abandoned the boat. Along with my family, I came with a friend from my hometown. Razban was the first person who jumped, crying 'Hell is empty, and all the devils are here'. I put my hand out to him, but the sea was too dark and oily, and he disappeared.

ARIEL *makes some notes in the book, and as he writes a group of the shipwreck's dead become spirits and perform 'Hey You' by Nima Yushij, with some lines also read by the ensemble and other refugees. As the spirits rise up,* ARIEL *directs some lines to Australia via journalists by speaking into the microphone.*

ARIEL/REFUGEES: 'Hey, you over there
who are sitting pleasantly on the shore,
bread on your tablecloths, clothes on your bodies,
someone is calling you from the water.
He beats the heavy wave with his tired hand,
his mouth agape, eyes torn wide with terror,
he has seen your shadows from afar,
has swallowed water in the dark blue deep,
each moment his impatience grows.

...
Hey you there,
he still has his eyes on this old world from afar,
he's shouting and hopes for help.
Hey you there
who are calmly watching from the shore,
the wave beats on the silent shore, spreads
like a drunk fallen on his bed unconscious,
recedes with a roar, and this call comes from afar again:
Hey, you over there ... '

ARIEL: [*to group*] Ehsan will escape tomorrow to draw attention to our plight. Some journalists already know. Keep it quiet for as long as you can.

ARIEL *closes the book and the refugees disperse.*

ACT TWO: AIR AND FIRE

SCENE ONE

June 2012. Eighteen months after the shipwreck. CALIBAN *addresses the audience.*

CALIBAN: Let me bring you to where the crabs grow. The crabs are my friends. Ever since I was a kid, I could make a crab stop moving. Just by talking to it. No-one else can do that.

Before this, I was a ranger. Professional crab-minder. At the end of each shift, you tally up the number of crab deaths. There are huge fines if a crab dies on your watch. I'd update the tally every day on the community noticeboard, and everyone comes past to have a look, and I'd hear about it if I wasn't looking after my crabs properly.

Mum used to worry about me. I mucked up a lot in school. When I was there, which wasn't a lot. The kids would give me a hard time. Say I couldn't speak English or read. Which I can. I'd just get nervous around the other kids, and clam up.

At school, there was a navy brat who wouldn't shut up about Mum. So I nicked a filleting knife from the fish shop. It's for delicate fish, so it's a long, thin knife. Very sharp. I took it to school in my backpack and watched him. I saw him leave class and followed him to the bathrooms. While he was washing his hands, I came up behind him and rested my knife on his temple, so he could see it in the mirror. He starts freaking out, yelling, telling me to let him go. I don't say anything. No-one's gonna hear him in this part of the school. I don't stab him. I'm not an idiot. I'm still not saying anything to the little prick. And then I just nick a bit of the top of his ear off. It's painful, and the jalang kecil (little bitch) squeals. But it's not so bad that it's obvious it's from a knife. I rinse the knife and I leave. And I don't hear much from him after that.

The day they arrived, the wind was pushing the boat towards the rocks. I called to the wind 'Push them towards the beach' and the wind shrieked back 'No, they belong to the water, not the land'.

The jungle grabbed me as I ran down to the beach, me pushing it back with my machete, praying to the spirits. 'Be at peace. Do not take more unhappy souls. Blessings to those in between.' But they didn't listen.

I don't like worrying Mum with work crap. But I told her a bit. How this job makes me feel like those shit teachers and kids from school. Random rules. Who's in, who's out. Hurting people to show you're in charge. I say 'Mum, this job is gonna kill me'. And she says what she always says. 'Stay out of trouble, son.'

I asked the sea, 'Do the people in the camp belong to the land or to you?' The sea laughed at me like Miranda does when I'm not getting something. 'That is the wrong question', said the sea.

SCENE TWO

The next day. Prospero's quarters.

MIRANDA: I don't want to be here when you discuss centre matters, I told you.

PROSPERO: He serves in offices that profit us, but you need to witness how to properly deal with the creature. Your affection is too humble.

CALIBAN *enters.*

Treacherous devil, you're in trouble.

CALIBAN: Figured as much.

CALIBAN *looks at* MIRANDA *nervously.*

PROSPERO: Don't look at my daughter.

CALIBAN: [*mumbling*] I'll look where I want.

PROSPERO: What? Speak English, we can't understand you.

Beat.

You hid a crab in my bed.

CALIBAN: Did it bite you like I told it to?

PROSPERO: It nearly took my finger off.

CALIBAN: [*laughing*] I thought I picked a good one! [*To* MIRANDA] It was the size of a whale shark.

MIRANDA: Why did you put a crab in his bed?

CALIBAN: Those crabs, scavenging the rubbish, they're the real survivors. He needed a reminder that some things came before him on this island.

PROSPERO: Caliban disagreed with a decision I made, and instead of discussing it, the detested slave—

CALIBAN: When you were first here, you made a big deal of me. Told me how useful I was, how nobody knew the island like I did. I foraged all the rare food for you that not even the whites get.

PROSPERO: And so you did. And now I know the island more intimately than you.

Beat.

You're supposed to be looking after my daughter.

MIRANDA: He has—

PROSPERO: She's sunburnt. Why is she getting sunburnt walking to and from school?

CALIBAN: Dunno. The sun here, it's intense.

PROSPERO: Well, it's your job to protect her.

MIRANDA: I'll wear a hat.

PROSPERO: Keep her on the shortest paths, look for shade. My daughter's skin is more delicate than yours, remember.

CALIBAN: I saved your daughter. On the beach when you arrived. You disappeared.

MIRANDA: I saved myself, Caliban. But you did get me medical attention quickly.

PROSPERO: My daughter has spoken. I owe you nothing. You should be grateful for the way I help the guards. I keep people calm and maintain order.

CALIBAN *goes to respond, looks at* MIRANDA *and stops.*

MIRANDA: The atmosphere at the centre troubles Father. If more escape like Ehsan …

PROSPERO: Don't waste your time trying to explain complex matters to him.

CALIBAN: There's nothing complex about people wanting to be dead instead of in this camp. You don't see them anymore.

PROSPERO: Caliban pretends to care for the people here. The pile of dirt makes trouble, that's all.

CALIBAN: How can a suicide attempt not be worth reporting?

PROSPERO: I've discussed my feedback with your boss. You were wrong to classify the incident as critical. It didn't succeed.

MIRANDA: Who was it?

PROSPERO: That's confidential. Miranda, get the locked case from my office.

MIRANDA *exits.*

You know if it was marked as critical, it would be reported, and she can be jailed? For the crime of attempting to take her own life.

CALIBAN: You think you're being a good guy?

PROSPERO: Can't you see, we are both this close to being cut off if they think we're not doing our jobs properly? Suicide attempts … And now Ehsan …

CALIBAN: Do you know where he's hiding? Are you protecting him?

PROSPERO: Make sure he is hunted soundly.

MIRANDA *re-enters with case.*

This will shake your shaking, I can tell you. You cannot tell who's your friend.

PROSPERO *opens the case.*

A gift. Special hooked knife. Next time someone tries to hang themselves, cut them down, don't report it. Your boss agrees with me.

CALIBAN: I'm not using a knife on people, you dog. This place makes soft people's heads go funny / Island fever.

MIRANDA: My father is of a better nature than he appears—

PROSPERO: Of course I have island fever. Your precious island with its stinking air and population of failures. You and your mother, gathering scraps like the crabs and thinking it's a life. You will do what I tell you to. You are nothing to them, lower than an illegal immigrant.

CALIBAN: I don't need your poxy knife. I've got plenty of them.

PROSPERO: I'm not afraid of you.

CALIBAN: It won't be a crab in your bed next time.

PROSPERO: All you're doing is worrying my daughter. I'm finished with you

CALIBAN: [*to* MIRANDA] He's composed of harshness. But if you're standing there listening to it, you're no better. He doesn't care about anyone else. Doesn't it worry you that he left you to drown?

MIRANDA: [*to* PROSPERO] Everyone deserves dignity. That's what you used to say to me.

PROSPERO: Don't narrate our past. Do you think he's your equal?

MIRANDA: Not everyone can be squeezed dry like a sponge.

CALIBAN: Hell is empty and all the devils are here.

Exit CALIBAN.

MIRANDA: Is this what you meant when you promised a better life?

PROSPERO: I'll tell the officials not to worry, Miranda. A detainee wouldn't put their freedom at risk by becoming close to a guard. You'll tell me, won't you? If anyone shares anything with you about Ehsan.

MIRANDA: I won't hear anything. They know I'd tell you.

SCENE THREE

A vision of MIRANDA*'s. During this scene, characters are foregrounded momentarily, then dissolve according to* MIRANDA*'s attention, rapidly adopting and discarding roles.* MIRANDA *is at Esteri's grave. The storm returns to the breaking ship and a rippling army of crabs migrate across the island.*

MIRANDA: All lost! All lost! To prayers! All lost! Mercy on us! We split, we split!

ARIEL *is the element of air and* CALIBAN *the element of water, coaxing* MIRANDA *towards them.*

Two elements fought for me after the shipwreck. The water, roaring and brutal on the surface, underneath seductive and gentle. The toxic air rose from the island's mine, prickling my skin and holding me fast. But I am stronger than both.

PROSPERO *tries to grab his staff.*

[*To* PROSPERO] You do assist the storm!

PROSPERO: I am less afraid to be drowned than thou art. We are only safe here for as long as I have power.

MIRANDA: You told me the same thing at home. You failed us.

PROSPERO: We're alive. How many families we knew are dead now?

MIRANDA: We understood the danger there. Your slipperiness does not suit this climate.

PROSPERO: I do not look for reverence, but for love. And harborage for myself, our ships and people.

A traditional Iranian song (Gol Pari Joon / Ghasem Abadi / Larzaneh) begins playing and ARIEL *dances to it, as* CALIBAN *and* PROSPERO *drum on the floor.* MIRANDA *watches* ARIEL *for some time.* ARIEL *notices* MIRANDA *looking at him and pulls her towards him.* MIRANDA *initially dances, and then tries to bring him back towards Esteri's grave, which he resists.*

MIRANDA: Bia baash harf bezan. (Come and speak to her.)
ARIEL: Nemikham, Miranda. (I don't want to, Miranda.)
MIRANDA: Shafa mideh. (It will heal you.)
ARIEL: I've already said goodbye to her.

The music stops abruptly.

MIRANDA: [*to* ARIEL] I am only safe if my faith in my father is completely believable. [*To audience*] He has a talent for discarding people. Caliban. Ehsan. The people still waiting back in Indonesia. As a motherless child, I am vulnerable, not spoiled.

MIRANDA *transitions to a narrated tableau.*

'There was a king whose comely daughter's grace
Was such that any man who glimpsed her face
Declared himself in love.'
CALIBAN: 'From his arrested hand the crust he ate
Dropped unregarded, and the princess smiled.
The glance lived in his heart—the man grew wild
With ardent love, with restless misery.'
MIRANDA: '"O wretched man"
She said, "How could you hope for love between
A dervish and the daughter of a queen?
You cannot live outside my palace door;
Be off with you and haunt these streets no more".'
[*To* ARIEL] Ariel. Tell Father what Caliban tried to do.

As air, ARIEL *whispers into* PROSPERO*'s ear and activates* CALIBAN.

PROSPERO: [*to* CALIBAN] You tried to violate the honour of my child.

PROSPERO *moves to strike* CALIBAN *with his staff.* MIRANDA *wrenches the staff from* PROSPERO *and beats* CALIBAN *with it.*

MIRANDA: Hated slave, which any print of goodness will not hold. Vile race, incapable of change. You deserve to be trapped on this island prison.

CALIBAN: Ahli sihir gila! (Crazy witch!) You led me on, stuck-up bitch! I am subject to a tyrant, a sorcerer, that by his cunning has cheated me of this island.

PROSPERO: For this, treacherous devil, be sure tonight you will have cramps, side stitches that will squeeze your breath from your body. You will be pinched as thickly as honeycomb, each touch more stinging than bees.

As PROSPERO *casts his spell,* CALIBAN *writhes on the floor in pain. The marching crabs rise up.*

I will fill your bones with aches, will make you roar so loudly your crabs will shake at the noise.

CALIBAN: This island's mine, and you've taken it from me. [*Commanding* ARIEL] The poisoned wind blow on you, and blister you all over!

As air, ARIEL *goes to attack* PROSPERO, *and* MIRANDA *restrains him using* PROSPERO*'s staff.*

MIRANDA: Enough! I will untie the spell.

MIRANDA *places* PROSPERO*'s cloak on* CALIBAN *to reverse the spell.*

Caliban never knowingly does wrong.

PROSPERO: Silence! One word more will make me scold you, if not hate you. An advocate for this imposter? Foolish wench, you have not seen enough men.

MIRANDA: Enough to recognise a true soul.

CALIBAN: No power on earth could make me leave this place,
But since your servants want to murder me,
Explain the meaning of this mystery:
Why did you smile at me that day?

MIRANDA: '"Poor fool,
I smiled from pity, almost ridicule—
Your ignorance provoked that smile." She spoke
And vanished like a wisp of strengthless smoke.'

The crabs become still. The scene shifts to a wedding between MIRANDA *and* ARIEL, *with* PROSPERO *officiating.*

PROSPERO: Look down ye gods and on this couple drop
A blessed crown, quiet days, fair issue and long life.
Give me your hands, and by the merry rite of spring
I charge you lovers you are eternally knit.

The music resumes. ARIEL *breaks away and continues dancing while* MIRANDA *addresses the audience.*

MIRANDA: Elusive air. Using me so enchantingly. Keeping me just close enough. Thinking I can be bent to your spirit.

MIRANDA *places the cloak on* PROSPERO *so he can longer see or hear.*

[*To* CALIBAN] You didn't imagine it. I enjoyed kissing you.

ARIEL *approaches* MIRANDA, *and* MIRANDA *pushes him away with magic.*

CALIBAN: So why are you choosing Ariel?

MIRANDA: You both threaten my destiny in Australia.

CALIBAN: Prospero's magic has ruined this place. Let him go. Stay here with me.

ARIEL: [*shouts over the music*] What are you saying?

ARIEL *and* MIRANDA *dance together.*

Have the Australians taught you what sitting on the fence is?

MIRANDA: You're asking for a betrayal.

ARIEL: It's punishing the government, not him.

MIRANDA: You're obsessed with the old music. You romanticise too much. It will be less charming as your hair turns grey.

ARIEL: Your father is sitting on the fence too.

MIRANDA: We've learned that's often the safest thing to do.

ARIEL: He likes his comforts here. Australia is too uncertain for him now.

MIRANDA: Everything is uncertain

CALIBAN *as water rushes towards her.* MIRANDA *stops him, keeping him at a distance.*

[*To* CALIBAN] You would drown me here, without meaning to.

While MIRANDA *is distracted,* ARIEL *moves towards the microphone.* MIRANDA *intercepts him before he can speak to Australia.* CALIBAN *recedes.*

ARIEL: [*to* MIRANDA] This island has corrupted your father.

ARIEL *pulls* MIRANDA *towards him in an invitation. The music and dancing stops abruptly and* CALIBAN *and* PROSPERO *exit,* PROSPERO *leaving his cloak behind.* MIRANDA *and* ARIEL *have returned to the present moment on the island.*

MIRANDA: It's not the island.

ARIEL: Have the Australians taught you 'being taken down a peg or two'?

MIRANDA: Related to being 'hung out to dry'? You are bound to him by an oath of allegiance.

ARIEL: You will never reach Australia if you let him continue. It's too risky for them to let him go. They're using him, and he is running out of things to give.

ARIEL *calls out to the refugees in the camp.*

My former master through his art foresees the danger. We must act quickly. It is a custom of Prospero's in the afternoon to sleep. Remember first to possess his book, for without it he is nothing. His power as holder of your stories, and portrayer of your case, is fading. It is time to advocate in our own voices.

MIRANDA: I won't let you take his book. You'll need more than that. Prove to me that our people are with you. I will keep the book safe during the riot.

ARIEL *exits.*

SCENE FOUR

Night at the camp the next day. PROSPERO *addresses the group of mourning refugees.* ARIEL *holds a white funeral shroud.*

PROSPERO: I am grieving with you for Ehsan. He was loved by all of us for his passion and his fierce loyalty to this group. Let us honour him. Born in Tabriz, he expected like his parents he would work in an automobile manufacturing factory. But destiny had other plans. A brilliant student, he went to study in Tehran, where he met his wife Roya. He started a promising career, and two beautiful children followed, Navid and Ismenia. But like many of us, his dreams for life in his home country turned to ash. Ehsan's death reminds us of the risks we take when we become impatient. Australia will never accept us if we don't abide by their laws. But I know we all know how to be patient.

ARIEL: We've been patient for long enough.

Protestors cheer.

We've been patient long enough. We came here to change our lives.

ARIEL *performs a whirling dervish dance to music, entering into an ecstatic trance state and unleashing the jinn spirits in the camp. Fires burn and a green phosphorescent haze hangs in the air.*

Blow, winds, and crack your cheeks. Rage, blow! You cataracts and hurricanes, spout till you have drenched our camp and drowned the raging red crabs. I call on the jinn spirits of the island.

ARIEL *grabs the microphone and speaks to journalists through the perimeter fence.*

By protesting, we are honouring the life of Ehsan, whose body was found at the bottom of the cliffs yesterday.

Do not believe the lies that he took his life. He was fighting for his freedom to the end, and this treacherous island and government took it from him.

People are sick of our truth not being believed, sick of arguing with immigration, sick of talking about compassion. It's time to join together and disband the camps. Or we'll have more refugees dying in offshore prisons.

ARIEL *leads a call and response with the other refugees.*

Freedom! High day!

REFUGEES: High day! Freedom!

ARIEL: Free refugees!

REFUGEES: Free refugees!

ARIEL: [*repeating until interrupted*] The world's watching!

REFUGEES: [*repeating until interrupted*] The world's watching!

PROSPERO *speaks to the journalists through the fence.*

PROSPERO: Enough. Enough. That's enough. You are not animals. Do not feed the stereotypes. Behave with some dignity.

PROTESTOR ONE: Tell us what you did to Ehsan.

PROSPERO: Nothing was done to Ehsan.

PROTESTOR TWO: Boroba! (Rubbish!) You and the government murdered him.

PROSPERO: [*to journalists*] What happened to Ehsan was very sad.

> ARIEL *speaks into the microphone to journalists, before being intercepted by* PROSPERO.

ARIEL: To the people up there running this camp, this is your fault. It is a dark power to control where and how people can live—

PROSPERO: Ariel has a very pure heart. I love him like a son. [*To refugees*] But he is playing heroics with your future. It's time to extinguish the fires. Put down your weapons.

ARIEL: Prospero has become disconnected from our people.

PROSPERO: I have known betrayal in my life before. It never surprises me.

ARIEL: You betrayed all of us long ago when you traded your people for a fibro house. I would rather live in my stinking container than enforce this regime.

PROSPERO: Australia is right there, we just need to hang on.

CALIBAN: They can't hang on anymore. We're meant to be looking after people, and they're dying. Ehsan died because you cast him out.

ARIEL: You hold powerful magic, Prospero. But not as powerful as you need it to be. I have a better patron now. One who might actually secure freedom for my family.

PROSPERO: You think some activist reporter will get you out of here? Always this selfish impatience! Who insisted we stop here rather than Darwin? Who brought us here?

> *A cavernous silence.*

ARIEL: You're right, Prospero. We should have sailed to Darwin.

PROSPERO: Your guilt, like a poison given to work a great time after, now begins to bite your spirit. And we suffer. Because you sell our stories cheaply to greedy journalists. Disband the jinn spirits, Ariel.

> PROSPERO *pulls the cord on the microphone to disconnect it. A jarring shriek of audio feedback, and the journalists and protestors disperse.* PROSPERO *and* ARIEL *are left alone.*

Deevoneh shodi? (Have you gone mad?) / Chi kar mikoni? (What are you doing?)

ARIEL: I had to, Prospero. Your way wasn't working.

PROSPERO: Two months. Two months I had our wait down to, before this disaster.

ARIEL: A remedy after death. We have harmed rather than healed. I know you've started feeding people's secrets to the government. I know you betrayed Ehsan. I'm not going to help you anymore.

PROSPERO: You've threatened my freedom, your freedom, Miranda's freedom. I'm going to be forced into a position where I'm going to have to cut you loose. For Miranda's sake.

ARIEL *begins exiting.*

And if I cut you loose, I'm cutting you.

ARIEL: We both have to do what we think is best for our families.

PROSPERO: Where is your family? You have no idea, do you?

PROSPERO *is left alone.*

'Who is like me, alone, in solitude,
Parched in the ocean's watery plenitude?
I've no one with me who might comprehend
My confidences, no one who's a friend;
I've no encouragement, and no defence
Against the darkness's malevolence.'

ACT THREE: EARTH

SCENE ONE

Two days after the riot. ARIEL *and* CALIBAN *are together in lockdown.*

CALIBAN: Worth it?

ARIEL: Probably not. Misery acquaints a man with strange bedfellows.

CALIBAN: I copped it from Mum. She'd heard all about it. Told me not to bother coming home.

ARIEL *reveals a paper bag.*

ARIEL: I smuggled something in. My vice.

CALIBAN: What's that?

ARIEL: It's toot. Rosewater-flavoured almond paste. My wife used to make it.

CALIBAN: How did you get it?

ARIEL: Miranda made it for me. Toot promises a life full of sweetness. Do you want some?

CALIBAN: No. I've got some news from camp. Not sure if you already heard.

ARIEL: Roya?

CALIBAN: When she heard the news about Ehsan. I went in to check on her, and …

ARIEL: If people think it's their time, then … there's nothing you can do.

CALIBAN: It wasn't the first time. I found her trying to do the same thing. Last time Ehsan was disciplined. She doesn't speak English, so I couldn't help much. Prospero wouldn't let me report it.

Beat.

I found a letter in Roya's quarters.

CALIBAN *fishes around in his clothes.*

It's here somewhere.

ARIEL: [*produces letter*] This letter?

CALIBAN: You nicked that out of my bag!

ARIEL: I don't want other guards seeing this.

CALIBAN: I kept it so her children don't find it.

ARIEL: I wonder if they'll bury her and Ehsan's bodies together. I can't eat this anymore.

ARIEL *sets the toot aside.*

CALIBAN: Another letter to add to your collection for Australia?

ARIEL: I'll burn it when we get out of here.

CALIBAN: A dead woman's final words, what's wrong with you? Give it here.

ARIEL *passes the letter to* CALIBAN.

May the wandering spirits move through to the next realm. Blessings for everyone's safety. Blessings to those in between.

ARIEL *joins* CALIBAN *in the chant, both holding the letter.*

ARIEL/CALIBAN: May the wandering spirits move through to the next realm. Blessings for everyone's safety. Blessings to those in between.

CALIBAN: Will Miranda and Prospero leave?

ARIEL: Even your beloved crabs sense when it is time to move on.

CALIBAN: Here's my comfort.

CALIBAN *gets out a hip flask and skolls.*

She's been such a big part of my life here. Then poof, gone. It'll be back to wild Caliban, roaming the jungle with my machete, getting into trouble.

CALIBAN *makes a retching noise.*

ARIEL: Are you unwell?

CALIBAN *shakes his head and takes another big swig from his flask, then lies down.*

CALIBAN: Sometimes I hear a thousand twanging instruments hum at my ears, and sometimes voices that send me back to sleep even if I had just woken up. Then I dreamed of clouds opening up and dropping such riches on me that when I woke up, I cried to dream again.

ARIEL *goes over to* CALIBAN *to assist.*

Leave me. Sometimes I am set upon by snakes, who with forked tongues hiss me into madness.

ARIEL: [*sniffing*] You smell like …

ARIEL *smells the hip flask.*

Bleach.

CALIBAN: He that dies pays all debts.

CALIBAN *starts convulsing.*

ARIEL. Help! He's poisoned himself! He's drunk bleach! Help!

Sirens wail and blue lights flash for code blue. THE POLITICIAN *(Peter Dutton) speaks as* ARIEL *moves* CALIBAN *into the recovery position.*

THE POLITICIAN: I have previously expressed my frustration and anger at advocates and others who are in contact with those in regional processing centres and who are encouraging some of these people to behave in a certain way, believing that the pressure exerted on the Australian Government will see a change in our policy in relation to our border protection measures.

MIRANDA *enters, carrying a bottle of ointment and a feather, dips the feather and traces it across* CALIBAN*'s torso.* CALIBAN*'s body relaxes, and* MIRANDA *presses the package of toot into his hand.*

ARIEL: [*to audience*] The loyal simurgh bird, protector of the outcasts, heard the lonely Caliban's cries and arose from the ash of the mine. It spread its copper wings and called to Miranda to follow, giving her a magical ointment, made of a mother's love, that was a salve to all sickness.

MIRANDA: [*to audience*] When the life came back into Caliban's body, the simurgh bird wept at the nearness of the shadow for Caliban, for there had been too much suffering on the island. She mourned those she had not been able to save, and her cries echoed around the island. No more, she called, no more.

SCENE TWO

A few hours later. PROSPERO, ARIEL *and* MIRANDA *in Prospero's house following an interview with the official.*

PROSPERO: Ariel, this is still fixable, for us. The people in the camp, they have no sense of loyalty. People will always try and tear leaders down, it's happened to me in my life before, you know that.

ARIEL: Tall poppy syndrome. That's what they call it here.

PROSPERO: Exactly. That interview went well, but there's no guarantee. We need Caliban to take some responsibility. Make an example of him.

MIRANDA: Babayee (Father), he nearly died. / He doesn't mean that, Ariel.

ARIEL: Shameful. / That sad young man. / We're not doing that, Prospero.

PROSPERO: When you've seen more of life Miranda, you'll understand. You have the virtue of compassion, don't take it too far.

MIRANDA: You have to stop punishing him for caring so much.

PROSPERO: You want to stay here with him, is that right? People this island with little Calibans?

MIRANDA: Babayee (Father), I am trying to get us to Australia.

PROSPERO *drains his coffee and places it down.*

PROSPERO: My book. I know one of you has stolen it. I need it back now.

ARIEL: We should never have started it. Storing people's secrets, screening their histories.

PROSPERO: Where is my book, Ariel? Miranda, do you know where Ariel has hidden my book?

MIRANDA: No, Father.

PROSPERO: Ariel, I've looked after you and your family the whole time you've been here. Give me the book. On Esteri's life—

MIRANDA: Stop. I took the book.

PROSPERO: Did Ariel tell you to?

MIRANDA: No. These stories, they haven't helped us. It would be better to just let people advocate for themselves, telling the truth.

PROSPERO: You think you know more than me now? Bring me the book, Miranda.

MIRANDA *exits and returns with the book.*

[*To* ARIEL] This is your doing. Somehow you put this in her head and tried to turn my child against me.

MIRANDA: He didn't. Not a child.

PROSPERO *discards the book.*

PROSPERO: And even now, I'm trapped in this cell.

MIRANDA: What does your coffee cup say?

PROSPERO: The shapes are blurry. My old bones ache today.

MIRANDA: Pass it to me.

MIRANDA *studies the cup.*

I see another journey. Calmer this time. A cave opening up. A release. Daybreak.

PROSPERO: All that in a little coffee cup. They're not going to let me go.

MIRANDA: Ariel, time for Hafiz.

ARIEL *picks up Fal-e Hafiz.* PROSPERO *closes his eyes and opens the book at a particular page, passing it to* ARIEL.

ARIEL: Let's see what you have.

'If there's no golden treasure, at least satisfied I remain
He who gave that to the king, made this the lot of the knave.
This world, just like a bride, in appearance is glorified
He who gave his life to this, has only dug his own grave.'

PROSPERO: That seems clear.

ARIEL: I haven't finished.

'From now on, I spend my time in nature with rivers and trees
While the breeze, of time of spring, would rant and rave.'

ARIEL *closes the book.*

The rarer action is in virtue than in vengeance. You're more dangerous to the government here. Plead ignorance with the riot. Go to Australia with Miranda.

SCENE THREE

One month later. CALIBAN *is lying down with a damp cloth over his eyes.* MIRANDA *is sitting near him, flicking through a book.*

MIRANDA: 'Why are you so enchanted by this world, when a mine of gold lies within you?'

Beat.

This is unbearable.

CALIBAN: You're meant to feel sorry for me. One more.

MIRANDA: 'Very little grows on jagged rock. Be ground. Be crumbled, so wild flowers will come up where you are.' Are you jagged rock, Caliban?

CALIBAN: I thought you'd like reading Rumi.

MIRANDA: He's Father's guide, not mine. We would have been safe at home if we weren't Sufis. So this all started with Rumi, really.

CALIBAN: Sorry. I just though he was Instagram famous.

MIRANDA: It doesn't matter. This will all be gone soon. Everyone's going to Villawood prison.

CALIBAN *goes to sit up while taking the cloth off his eyes.*

CALIBAN: Are you going?

MIRANDA: Back down.

CALIBAN *lies back.*

No, we've been granted asylum. Time for Australia. Finally.

CALIBAN: Are you sure?

MIRANDA: That's what Father said.

CALIBAN: You should ask for the paperwork. Double check.

MIRANDA: We won't be able to leave without it.

CALIBAN: You'll be stuck with just him in Australia.

MIRANDA: We've been together for a long time. I'm used to it.

CALIBAN: Whatever Australia has to offer, Christmas Island has as much to offer.

MIRANDA: You'll have to leave one day. Can you see yet?

CALIBAN: Not yet. Doctor said it won't be long.

MIRANDA: What would your Mum have done if you'd died?

CALIBAN: She'd have sued them. She knows how to look after herself. There might still be a workers comp in it for me. If my eyes fix up, they're letting me stay here. Hot contingency.

MIRANDA: What do you mean?

CALIBAN: That's what they're doing. Emptying it, but keeping some of us employed. Just in case.

MIRANDA: You must leave.

CALIBAN: I've got no skills, no training. What I must do is have a job.

MIRANDA: It'll kill you.

CALIBAN: It'll be better now. No people. Just the buildings and crabs again.

MIRANDA: That's what you should be doing, Caliban. Working with crabs again. And then moving on like your crabs once the season's changed.

CALIBAN: I can't be a crab-sitter for the rest of my life. And Mum's here. It's a special place to live, you haven't seen half of it—

MIRANDA: Thank you for helping me on the beach when I arrived.

CALIBAN: If it hadn't been me, it would have been someone else.

MIRANDA: I don't think so.

CALIBAN: Don't listen to the local chat. People go a bit crazy being on an island after a while, they don't mean half the stuff they say about you lot. You could get to know people here.

MIRANDA: You're too good for this island. There's so many things that only you can do—

CALIBAN: Don't say stuff because you feel sorry for me.

MIRANDA: There's a difference between pity and care.

Beat.

Our revels now are ended. All will dissolve, and like this insubstantial pageant faded, leave not a rack behind.

CALIBAN: I wish you belonged here.

MIRANDA: I don't.

CALIBAN: I'm just not sure if you belong on the mainland either.

SCENE FOUR

The next morning.

MIRANDA: Happiness! Sunrise on a new day! We are finally going to Australia! O wonder! A brave new world! How beautiful mankind is!

PROSPERO: I forget it's new to you.

MIRANDA: This whole time we've been living a half-life, a waiting life. It doesn't feel safe to hope.

PROSPERO: Dear heart. You rub the sore, when you should apply the bandage. Think of this as a bad dream. Real life starts tomorrow.

MIRANDA: Will we live near Bondi Beach?

PROSPERO: We'll be assigned temporary accommodation while I look for work. I might drive taxis for a bit.

MIRANDA: But Babayee (Father) … after the temporary accommodation, we might live near Bondi?

PROSPERO: Haven't you had enough of the sea?

MIRANDA: I can't go on a boat again.

PROSPERO: Just a short trip to the mainland. Then we'll fly. I promise you calm seas, auspicious gales.

MIRANDA: If only you could control the weather.

MIRANDA *passes* PROSPERO *the book of refugees' stories.*

PROSPERO: You must prepare yourself. To be poorly treated.

MIRANDA: In what way?

PROSPERO: For people like us, there will always be more freedom in in-between spaces. We will not enjoy the privileges that my role afforded us here.

MIRANDA: Babayee (Father). I'm sorry for taking your book.

PROSPERO: No word of apology from you. Dokhmal, you saved me. When I felt like I couldn't carry our burdens any longer, you would smile at me, or show some small kindness to others, and that sustained my spirits. And now you will have a safe home.

Beat.

Before we leave, I have one final task. [*Motioning to book*] No more magic.

MIRANDA: A new beginning?

'Knowing love's ocean is a shoreless sea,
What help is there?—abandon life, and founder
When you give your heart to love, you make the moment lucky:
No need of auguries to perform good deeds.'

They embrace. PROSPERO *exits with his staff and draws a circle on the ground. While speaking,* PROSPERO *breaks his staff in half and places it in the circle.*

PROSPERO: I have charmed the kings of this island, drawn forth secrets with my staff, whipped up and quieted discontent and drawn open then closed the curtains of people's eyes. But this rough magic I here abjure. I break my staff, bury it certain fathoms in the earth, and deeper than plummeted sound I'll drown my book.

PROSPERO *performs 'The Strangers' Case' extract from* Sir Thomas More *by Shakespeare into the microphone to Australia, with individual refugees and the ensemble also performing some lines.*

PROSPERO/REFUGEES: Imagine that you see the wretched strangers,

Their babies at their backs and their poor luggage,
Plodding to the ports and coasts for transportation,
And that you sit as kings in your desires,
Authority quite silent by your brawl,
And you in ruff of your opinions clothed;
What had you got? I'll tell you: you had taught
How insolence and strong hand should prevail,
How order should be quelled; and by this pattern
Not one of you should live an aged man,
For other ruffians, as their fancies wrought,
With self same hand, self reasons, and self right,
Would shark on you, and men like ravenous fishes
Would feed on one another …
Whither would you go?
What country, by the nature of your error,
Should give you harbor?
… Would you be pleased
To find a nation of such barbarous temper,

That, breaking out in hideous violence,
Would not afford you an abode on earth,
Whet their detested knives against your throats,
Spurn you like dogs, and like as if that God
Owed not nor made not you …
What would you think
To be thus used? This is the strangers' case;
And this your mountainish inhumanity.

PROSPERO: [*to book*] I return you to Flying Fish Cove.

The refugees join the book in the circle. It begins to rain. THE POLITICIAN *(Jacqui Lambie) speaks.*

THE POLITICIAN: What kind of message are we frightened of sending? That if we show a little bit of kindness … then other people will look at that and go 'I'll sign up for the same'. They'll all make the life-threatening trip across the ocean in a sinking boat. They'll all arrive in Australia, try and put down some roots, get put in detention, get put in detention in another place. They'll all sign up to be left there until their own child's blood turns to poison in their veins … And I don't know how you look at those two girls in the eye and tell them 'Hey, sorry sweethearts, it's nothing personal, it's not your fault, but there is no home here for you'. Priya and Nades are not owed our protection, but just because we don't owe them this little bit of mercy, doesn't mean we can't offer it to them.

DIVE-SHOP OWNER *enters.*

DIVE-SHOP OWNER: [*to audience*] So just doing a spot of expectation management here, folks. Obviously the weather's gone troppo out of nowhere, especially around Flying Fish Cove, so sunset drinks will now be inside. Water glimpses, is how those in the real estate business might describe the view. Don't throw your neck out craning to see it. I've got some spare lifejackets—does anyone want them for the boat back?

PROSPERO: And now my charms are all o'erthrown, And what strength I have's mine own, which is most faint now, 'tis true—

DIVE-SHOP OWNER: Move along please, you're scaring the tourists. Crazy Leb talking to himself.

PROSPERO: Crazy Iranian. Iranian-Australian.

DIVE-SHOP OWNER: Well, fuck off home, then, people are already wanting a refund because of all this.

He gestures to the weather.

Safe travels, boss.

PROSPERO *and* DIVE-SHOP OWNER *exit in different directions.* ARIEL *enters, trying to avoid the group of tourists.*

Oi! Here's trouble!

ARIEL: Well, they agreed with your assessment.

DIVE-SHOP OWNER: Off to Villawood? You've got some fight left, I can tell.

THE POLITICIAN: When you give something away, and it's not out of obligation, that's what you call generosity. That's the Australian way.

DIVE-SHOP OWNER: [*gesturing to the audience*] C'mon, give them a try.

ARIEL: [*into microphone*] Good people of Australia.

Let me not, since I have pardon'd the deceiver, dwell in this bare island by your spell, but release me from my bands with the help of your good hands.

Now I lack spirits to enhance, art to enchant, and my ending is despair, unless I be relieved by prayer, which pierces so that it assaults mercy itself and frees all faults.

As you from crimes would pardon'd be, let your indulgence set me free.

ARIEL *bows to the audience's applause and exits.*

THE END

THE STREET PRESENTS

THIS ROUGH MAGIC

BY HELEN MACHALIAS

World Premiere Season at The Street Theatre, Canberra 11–19 November 2023

GOVERNMENT ACKNOWLEDGEMENTS

This project is made possible with the support of the ACT government.

THE STREET COMPANY

Artistic Director & CEO	Caroline Stacey OAM
Executive Producer	Dean Ellis
Arts Projects Coordinator	Eva Ross
Communications	Su Hodge
Customer Service & Ticketing	Pierce Craswell
Front of House	Eva Ross , Pierce Craswell, William Malam
Design	Design♡Cult

The Street Board

Mark Craswell (Chair), Susan Blain (Deputy Chair), Susana Fior (Treasurer), Penny Calvert, Christina Graves, Igor Kochovski

We acknowledge the Ngunnawal and Ngambri peoples as the Traditional Owners of the lands on which The Street Theatre stands and where we live and create. We recognise their continuing connection to land, waters, community and culture, and pay our respects to all First peoples, their Elders past and present.

The Street is an ACT Government Arts Centre managed by The Stagemaster Inc., a not-for-profit organisation. The Street is supported by the ACT government through artsACT.

CAST

In order of appearance

Prospero	George Kanaan
Ariel	Reza Momenzada
Miranda	Kaitlin Nihill
Caliban	Andre Le
Dive Shop Owner, Immigration Official, Parnia	Lainie Hart

Politicians, the chorus of Hungry Ghosts and Refugees are played by the ensemble.

CREATIVE TEAM

Direction	Beng Oh
Dramaturgy	Dr Rebecca Clode, Granaz Moussavi
Lighting Design	Gerry Corcoran
Production Design	Imogen Keen
Sound Design	Kyle Sheedy
Cultural Consultants	Sheida Jafari, Parastoo Seif

PRODUCTION TEAM

Stage Manager	Brittany Myers
Lighting Operator	William Malam
Sound Operator	Kyle Sheedy
Set Construction	AVL Australia
Production Crew	Gerry Corcoran, Darren Hawkins Connor McKay, William Malam
Publicity	Su Hodge
Marketing Artwork	Design♡Cult
Production Photography	Novel Photographic
Production Videography	Craig Alexander

SETTING

The action of *This Rough Magic* take place on Christmas Island between 2010 and 2012 in various locations including: the sea, the beach, an interview room, a cave, the detention centre, Prospero's quarters, the clifftops at Esteri's grave, under the forest canopy, a wild dream, in lockdown, Prospero's office and Flying Fish Cove.

FROM THE WRITER

The Tempest, with its themes of slavery, liberation and empathy, and the postcolonial readings that have been applied to it, made it a potent starting point for a play about refugees and offshore detention.

Once I'd chosen Christmas Island detention centre as the play's location, the story unfurled. The island's fascinating history has made it a central character of the work, including the symbiotic relationship between the detainees and locals and the heroic actions Christmas Islanders took on the day of the SIEV 221 shipwreck.

In telling this story, it was essential to me that the writing process placed the voices of people with lived experience in the foreground. I am grateful to The Street for facilitating this, particularly the insights from cultural consultants with experience of detention on Christmas Island.

This Rough Magic has evolved to become a genre-bending Shakespearean adaptation that is both a celebration of Shakespeare and an act of rebellion against the canon. Iranian culture, Farsi language and Persian myth and storytelling traditions are as prominent as the Shakespearean text, offering a countervailing perspective on what we think of as 'the classics'.

While this play starts with an event from 2010, the Christmas Island detention centre was in active use as I was writing this play, both to transfer refugees from the Australian mainland during the pandemic and to detain the Murugappan family. While the family returned to Biloela last year in response to a concerted public campaign, the reference to the Tamil family's case in the plays serves as a fitting reminder of Australia's current use of offshore detention. The Murugappan family's experience is emblematic of the profligacy and cruelty of Australia's immigration policies, but more positively, that the dogged determination of vocal communities can create enough pressure to make change.

Helen Machalias
October 2023

FROM THE DIRECTOR

We begin with Shakespeare. *The Tempest* is the lens through which we see the world of *This Rough Magic*. It follows that our production is Shakespeare inflected and likewise our credo: to evoke, not illustrate. From that starting point our journey through the play has taken us through Christmas Island, accounts of immigration detention, Persian culture, poetry, politics and more.

This Rough Magic is a full play. It's imaginative and ambitious and its language is rich and full of feeling. It isn't a documentary but it has an emotional truth. It brings together stories that we know, or think we know, and refashions them and makes them ours. It's an epic entertainment that is, in the end, an Australian story.

Beng Oh
Canberra October 2023

FROM THE ARTISTIC DIRECTOR

Over the last fifteen years The Street has worked to grow a space for the gathering of theatrical ideas and minds providing fertile ground for Canberra to develop a distinctive and strong voice that is part of our national conversation and cultural narrative. Producing contemporary Australian theatre in Canberra we pursue a theatre of ideas, inquiry and imagination that talks to who we are and the world around us. Intellectually provocative, politically challenging, morally complex, inventive storytelling using all the languages of theatre.

This Rough Magic was pitched to me by Helen in 2019 where she put forward her idea for an adaptation of The Tempest mixed with 2010 Christmas Island Boat Disaster – the Siev 221. Through our difficult pandemic years Helen wrote and re-wrote moving through developments on zoom and then in our rehearsal room with a wonderful mix of actors and creatives from across Australia to produce this remarkable work. I have admired her tenacity and capacity to absorb a huge range of critical responses to craft *This Rough Magic* and the thoughtful, caring and inspiring artists who have contributed to this brilliant re-imagining traversing Australia's history and our collective responsibility towards those with whom share the world.

Caroline Stacey OAM
Canberra October 2023

HELEN MACHALIAS
Playwright

Helen Machalias has previously worked with The Street Theatre to develop a stage adaptation of Robin Klein's *People Might Hear You*, as well as *In Loco Parentis*, which examined the cover-up of sexual harassment and assault on university campuses. *In Loco Parentis* premiered at The Street as part of the Made in Canberra program for the Centenary of Canberra and won a Canberra Critics Circle Award. Helen has worked with Sydney Theatre Company, Riverside Theatres and Playwriting Australia, and has been shortlisted three times for Sydney Theatre Company's Young Playwright of the Year Award. *This Rough Magic* is her first mainstage production.

BENG OH
Director

Beng Oh is a Melbourne based Asian-Australian director who's staged a wide range of productions. He's passionate about diversity, new work and queer theatre. Productions include *Porcelain* by Chay Yew (The Street Theatre), *The Six Guys an Immigrant Trans Person of Colour will date in Melbourne* by Dax Carnay (La Mama), *Soul of Possum* by Brodie Murray (YIRRAMBOI and Castlemaine State Festival), *Cock* by Mike Bartlett (Baker's Dozen), *Wild Cherries* by Daniel Keene (La Mama), *Coloured Aliens* by Chi Vu (La Mama), *The Yellow Wave* by Jane Miller (Poppyseed Festival and Regional Arts Victoria), *Mein Kampf* by George Tabori (La Mama and Fortyfivedownstairs) and the *Lotus Readings* for Playwriting Australia.

He trained at the Victorian College of the Arts and is a member of the Lincoln Center Theatre Directors Lab in New York. He is co-artistic director of 15 Minutes from Anywhere and is on the committee of management for La Mama Theatre. Beng is also an associate of Contemporary Asian Australian Performance.

GRANAZ MOUSSAVI
Dramaturg

Granaz Moussavi, a poet and filmmaker, was born in Tehran. Granaz studied drama in Tehran/Iran and continued her studies in Australia entering a BA course in Screen Studies in 1998; then finished an honours degree in Flinders University in 2002. She is a graduate from Postgraduate degree in film editing from Australian Film School (AFTRS) and in 2013 successfully completed a Doctorate in Film Studies and Filmmaking in University of Western Sydney with a thesis project on the aesthetics of poetic cinema. Granaz has made several short films and documentaries. Her debut feature film *My Tehran For Sale* (2009) won an Australian IF award for best independent film and was internationally premiered in Toronto Film Festival. Granaz has made her second feature film on location in Afghanistan: *When Pomegranates Howl* (2021) which has been the Australian entry to the Academy Awards in International section (foreign language) and Asia Pacific Screen Award nominee. This film premiered at the International Tokyo Film Festival.

REBECCA CLODE
Dramaturg

Dr Rebecca Clode is the Ethel Tory Lecturer in Drama at the Australian National University. Her research focuses on playwriting practices and Australian theatre history. Rebecca is a PhD graduate of the ANU and also holds an MA in Text and Performance Studies from King's College and the Royal Academy of Dramatic Art, London. Prior to her academic career, she was a theatre practitioner, and she now maintains her practice locally as a dramaturg for playwriting development projects.

GEORGE KANAAN
Actor

George is an actor living on the lands of the Dharug and Eora people. His theatre credits include: *Homebody/Kabul* (Downstairs Belvoir); *The Last Highway* (Urban Theatre Projects–Sydney Festival); *Mirage* and *Wasted* (Horizon Theatre); *Antony & Cleopatra* (Vantage Theatre); and *Summer Holiday and Toons on Vacation* (Saudi Arabia & Qatar). Feature films include *Stage 5 (Eddie Arya)*, and, *A War Story* as Osama bin Laden (John Laing).

Select short film credits include: *The Worst* (Sharon Mani); *Bani Ibrahim* (Raihan Harun); *Squalor* (Paul Barakat); and, *The Pizza* (Johnny Tran). George's TV work includes: *Bay of Fires*; *The Secrets She Keeps*; *Total Control*; *Bite Club*; *Hyde & Seek*; *All Saints*; and, *East West 101*, where he was a nominee for an AFI for Best Supporting/Guest Actor in a Television Drama. George has appeared in over a dozen television commercials and holds a B. Arts (Key Program in Psychology) with Dean's Medal. George contributed to the development of *This Rough Magic* and this is his debut with The Street Theatre.

REZA MOMENZADA
Actor

Reza Momenzada trained at The Actors Center and most recently played the role of Ali in Queensland Theatre Company's *First Casualty*. Other theatre credits include: *Gloria* (Outhouse Theatre); *The Humans* (The Old Fitz); and *The Sound of Waiting* (Darlinghurst Theatre Company). Reza was nominated at The Glug Awards for the Most Outstanding Performance for *The Sound of Waiting*.

Reza is from the Kabul region, the capital city of Afghanistan. He has also lived in Iran and Syria and his main languages are Farsi/Persian and Dari as well as some Arabic. Reza contributed to the development of *This Rough Magic* and this is his debut with The Street Theatre.

LAINIE HART
Actor

Lainie Hart recently appeared in productions of *The Children* and *Three Tall Women* (Chaika Theatre) and her theatre credits include: *The Importance of Being Earnest* (Everyman Theatre); *Steel Magnolias* (Free Rain Theatre); *God of Carnage* (Echo Theatre); *Rosencrantz & Guildenstern are Dead* (Canberra Repertory); and *Sounds of Shakespeare, Twelfth Night* (Lakespeare&Co). Live stream work includes: *Rockspeare Richard III* (Lakespeare & Co); *Leopoldville* (Canberra Theatre Centre); and *Stripped* (The Q). Lainie toured Victoria with *Playhouse Creatures* (Pigeonhole Theatre). She has worked with The Street Theatre on creative development projects for *First Seen - New Works in Progress*. Lainie spent 18 months completing further study and training where she graduated from the full-time program at *16th Street Actor's Studio* in Melbourne and went on to perform in the La Mama autumn season of *Survival*.

Lainie contributed to the development of *This Rough Magic* and this is his debut with The Street Theatre.

ANDRE LE
Actor

Andre's performing arts journey began in high school, studying piano and drama which landed him roles in school productions of *Red Noses*, The *Addams Family, And Then There Were None*.

Community theatre credits include: *Be More Chill* as Michael Mell for which he received a CAT Recognition of Excellence, *A Migrant's Son* (Budding Theatre). Andre has also appeared in commercial campaigns and various short films including Adventurers Wanted, Weather, The Everyday Life of William(Academy of Interactive Entertainment), Relationships for Dummies (CIT Screen and Media). Music Direction and repetiteur work includes: *The Hello Girls* (Heart Strings Theatre Company), *Downtown* (Queanbeyan Players);

Currently completing a Double Degree; Bachelor of Science (Psychology)/Music, *This Rough Magic* is his first professional role and debut with The Street Theatre.

KAITLIN NIHILL
Actor

Kaitlin is a performer with a Bachelor of Musical Theatre from the Queensland Conservatorium Griffith University and a Diploma of Musical Theatre from NIDA. She recently portrayed Louise in *The Hello Girls* (Heart Strings Theatre Company). While at the Conservatorium, Kaitlin played various roles including Emily in *Our Town*, Baby Rosie in *Babes in Arms*, and Mrs. Tottendale in *The Drowsy Chaperone*, and was cast as Glinda in *Wicked* (cancelled due to COVID-19). Kaitlin performed in the ensemble of *Chimerica* (Sydney Theatre Company) in 2017 while at NIDA. Kaitlin is also passionate about creating her own work and recently performed her cabaret *How I Love To Give Them Back* with original music by James Court and herself in '10 Act Cabaret' (Chapel Off Chapel). *This Rough Magic* is her debut with The Street Theatre.

IMOGEN KEEN
Costume and Set

Imogen Keen is an award-winning set and costume designer for professional theatre productions. She has enjoyed a long collaboration with The Street Theatre, including design for: *Art; Twenty Minutes With The Devil; Milk; Breaking The Castle; Flight Memory; Fragments; Metamorphosis; A Doll's House, Part 2; Venus in Fur; Diary of a Madman; The Weight of Light; Boys Will Be Boys; Under Sedation; Constellations; Cold Light; The Faithful Servant; The Chain Bridge; MP; Where I End & You Begin; The Give & Take; To Silence; Jacques Brel is Alive and Well and Living in Paris; Dido and Aeneas*. Imogen has received Canberra Critics Circle Awards for Theatre Design (2009; 2011) and an MEAA Peer Acknowledgement Award (2011). She has worked on a wide variety of theatre, film, music, and cross-disciplinary productions for numerous theatre companies. Imogen graduated from the ANU School of Art in 1993.

GERRY CORCORAN
Lighting

Gerry Corcoran is a Lighting Designer/Technician based in Wolumla, NSW and is originally from Scotland. Gerry has been Chief Electrician/Lighting Designer at Pitlochry Festival Theatre in the Scottish Highlands and Chief Electrician/Technical Training Tutor (Lighting) for the Royal Scottish Academy of Music Drama in Glasgow, for which he designed over 40 productions ranging from small one-person scenes to full scale opera.

Australian lighting design credits include: *Art; Breaking The Castle (LIT Lighting Design Award 2022), Milk, A Doll's House Part 2* (The Street Theatre); *The Iliad–Out Loud* (Four Winds Festival); *Mamma Mia!* (Dreamcoat Theatre Productions); *Ladies in Black* (Spectrum Theatre Group). Operating as GCLX: Gerry Corcoran Production Lighting, he provides support for all types of productions, performances and events in the Bega Valley and beyond.

KYLE SHEEDY
Sound

Kyle Sheedy is an Audio Engineer based in Canberra. With an Advanced Diploma in Sound Production through CIT. Predominately a live engineer working on festivals and local gigs, he also works in other areas of sound. He has worked on a range of films as Location Recordist and Boom Operator as well as Sound Editor, Designer and Mixer in Post Production. He also works in the recording studio with band Recordings, Mixing, Mastering, and other tasks such as Audio Restoration.

Sound design credits include *Constellations, Tourmaline, The War of The Worlds, Venus in Fur, Fragments* (The Street Theatre), *Drought and Other Plays By Millicent Armstrong* (Music Theatre Projects Ltd).

BRITTANY MYERS
Stage Manager

Brittany Myers graduated with a Bachelor of Communications (Theatre/Media) from Charles Sturt University. She works predominantly as a freelance stage manager, but also has credits as an actor, devisor, choreographer, and costumer.

Her theatre credits as Stage Manager include: *In His Words, Art, Twenty Minutes with the Devil, Milk* (The Street Theatre), *Victory Over the Sun* (The Street/National Gallery of Australia), *The Hello Girls* (Heart Strings Theatre Company), *Ruthless!* (Echo Theatre), *Puffs, This Changes Everything* (Echo Youth), *Act Up!* (Canberra Theatre Centre), *Shape of Things* (Lambert House Enterprises), *Good Morning* (The Old 505 Theatre), *Wunderage* (Circus Oz).

ABOUT THE STREET

The Street Theatre is Canberra's creative powerhouse of inquiry, ideas and imagination, currently led by acclaimed stage director Caroline Stacey OAM. An award-winning home of live performance in the ACT and a major investor in new theatre, music work and artists in Canberra over the last decade. The Street commissions, develops, produces and presents live performance that help us talk to who we are and the world around us. The Street believes in the remarkable capacity of Canberra artists to speak to our time, and the need for them to be given creative space to make work of vision, ambition, and courage that talks to diverse audiences across Australia.

Just as Canberra is considered a petri-dish for new policies, ideas and cultural products within the broader national landscape, The Street serves a vital role as a key creative generator of new work and regenerator of place and community within the nation's political heart. The Street was the recipient of a 2020 Sidney Myer Performing Arts Award for outstanding achievement and is an ACT Government Arts Centre and an essential contributor to the well-being of residents in the ACT and artistic vibrancy in the region.

WWW.THESTREET.ORG.AU

FIND US

Phone	(02) 6247 1519
Address	15 Childers Street Canberra City
Social	#thestreetcbr #thestreetART @thestreetcbr

Supported by

The Street is managed by The Stagemaster Inc., a not-for-profit organisation. The Street is supported by the ACT government through artsACT and is an ACT Government Arts Centre.

ACKNOWLEDGEMENTS

From The Street

The Street gives our thanks to the following artists for their generous and insightful contribution to the development of *This Rough Magic* over the last four years.

Actors
Rahel Alemseged
Arishia Bordbar
Linda Chen
Peter Cook
Raoul Craemer
Christina Falsone
Lainie Hart
Chelsea Healey
George Kanaan
Stefanie Lekkas
Reza Momenzada
Mark Salvestro
William Tran
PJ Williams
Joshua Wiseman

Dramaturgs
Granaz Moussavi
Rebecca Clode

Directors
Nicky Tyndale-Biscoe
Anna Johnstone

First Seen Program Producer
Shelly Higgs

Secondment – Assistent Dramaturgs
Marni Mount

Cultural Consultant
Yasin Sarabi

From The Writer

Helen Machalias

This Rough Magic was written on the traditional lands of the Ngunnawal and Ngambri people, and the Gadigal people of the Eora nation. I recognise their continuing connection to land, waters, and culture, and pay my respect to their Elders past and present.

Thank you to The Street Theatre team for supporting the development and production of *This Rough Magic* over many years, especially Shelly Higgs for her guidance during the First Seen program and other creative developments. My deep appreciation to Caroline Stacey for her belief in my work and her commitment to seeing *This Rough Magic* come to life on stage.

Thank you also to the many wonderful creatives who helped me shape the play over its three year development, in particular the two brilliant dramaturgs Granaz Moussavi and Dr Rebecca Clode. Thank you Naz for the generosity and trust you showed in sharing your deep knowledge with me, and Bec for your perceptive insights and encouragement.

Thank you to my family and friends, especially Rey, Alex, Mum and Dad for all your emotional and practical support – this wouldn't have been possible without you.

FIRST SEEN

FIRST SEEN

This Rough Magic was developed through The Street's First Seen Works-in-Progress Program.

PRODUCTION SPONSOR

We thank our Street Supporters for their donations supporting the production of new work grown and made in Canberra.

SCRIPT PUBLICATION

The Currency Press script and program is generously supported by Michael Sassella.

THE STREET DONORS

STREET-LIFE ($5,000+)
Michael Adena, Joanne Daly

STREET-PARTY ($1,000+)
Mark Craswell, Raoul Craemer, Colin Neave AM, Michael Sassella, Caroline Stacey OAM, David Williams, Cathy Winters, Peter Wise, Secret Admirers (2)

STREET-WORKS ($500+)
Joan Adler, Michele Foster, Jamie Hladky, Bridget Sack, Secret Admirer

STREET-STYLE ($250+)
Joanna Clay, Peter Cranston, George Lawrence, Ann Murn, Peta Spender, Dr Barrie Stacey, Ilona Di Bella, Secret Admirers (3)

STREET-WISE (UP TO $250)
Alex Agafonoff, Sharon Ball, Ian Batterham, Sue Beitz, Neville Bleakley, Kate Bosser, Catherine Bowman, Andrea Bryant, Rohan Buettel, Nancye Burkevics, Moria Byrne, Sarah Christopher, Andrea Close, Elizabeth Costell, Nooneee Doronila, William Fleming, Alan Flett, Simon Garcia, James Gary, Carey Gaul, Julian Gilchrist, Roger Gottlob, Elena Grigorieva, Cathy Harrison, David Hennessy, Su Hodge, Anne Holmes, Graeme Hoy, Gary James, Carol Kee, Alistair Korn, Lauretta Laurie, Choe Li , Adam Maples, Neil McAlister, Bronwyn McNaughton, Rosamund Murn, Chris Nobs, Cameron Ong, Think Place, Loretto Poerio, Maurice Pollock, Andrew Purdham, Linda Rossiter, Mandy Scott, Tobi Skerra, Adam Stankevicius, Sherene Suchy, Beng Tan, John Taverner, Paul Taylor, Randl Taylor, ThinkPlace, Amy Wang, Julia Wee, Rosemary White, Michelle Wilson, Secret Admirer (6)

F·R·I·E·N·D